ADVANCE PRAISE & TESTIMONIALS

"Dr. P is not only one of the coolest people I know, he is an amazing Performance Psychologist. He will teach you science and show you tools, but most of all, how to relax in daily, stress-filled environments. The dude has swag all around."

> —**Demarcus Ware, World Champion NFL Player**

"The goal of psychotherapy is to move what is unconscious to conscious. Dr. P helped me to develop insight into who I am as a person. The many conversations that we had helped me to become aware of who I am and who I want to be. My gratitude for his professional abilities is something that I remain appreciative of for life. His personal authenticity and ability to normalize counseling is what gives him a unique ability to help others transform. Many thanks for being there for me, I won't forget it."

> —**Julius Thomas, Psy. D. Candidate**
> **All Pro Football Player**
> **Denver Broncos, Jacksonville Jaguars, and Miami Dolphins**

"Dr. P is an amazing person. He is funny, smart, and insightful! He taught me techniques I had never been exposed to previously. My first season with him, we went 10–6 after some really bad years. I attribute much of my development to his techniques and teachings. Plus, the dude can dance!"

> —**Ryan Tannehill, Starting NFL Quarterback,**
> **Comeback Player of the Year 2019**

"Dr. P has added a whole new dimension to our radio show. His knowledge and insight into sports and psychology make him an unusual talent. In addition, he is a faithful and dedicated friend. Having known Rick Perea for the past eight years, I can tell you that it feels as if our friendship has lasted a lifetime. Rick has been with me through both times of joy and hardship, and after reading his book, you will come to feel that Rick is there for you, too."

—Sandy Clough, 40-year Veteran, Talk Radio

"Being a part of Dr. Perea's presentations is unlike any experience you've ever had. His passion for his work and helping others cultivates inspiration and motivation. Being the most energetic psychologist out there, he engages his audience and creates an interactive environment. His relatability and personalization attract others and captivates attention. Dr. Perea's presentations will challenge your way of thinking and will leave you in awe and inspired."

—Vivian Maza, Chief People Officer Ultimate Software

DECISION POINT

The Moment Leaders Are Born

*The Psychology of Leadership
in the Face of Trauma & Tragedy*

RICK PEREA, Ph.D.

Printed by ThinkOne, United States of America.
First printing, June 2020.

For permission requests, Send to:
Attention: Permissions Request
Dr. Rick Perea
6888 S. Clinton Street, Suite 102
Greenwood Village, CO 80112
www.THINKONE4YOU.org

Front cover image by Monique Olson Photography
Author Coaching & Book Design:
Jacqueline Arnold
www.sweetlifeusa.com

Dedication

I dedicate this book to my brother Danny and also to my dear friend Alexis "Lexy" Keith, both murdered and taken too soon. Your lives were cut way too short, but your legacies live on through the impression you each made on my heart and the hearts of those who knew you. You both were my pure inspiration to write this book; your lives and your absences inspire me to live life at 212°. We miss you more than words can describe; you live on through us every day. It's also dedicated to my Dad, Rudolpho Victoriono Perea, THE TITAN. Dad may you rest in peace and enjoy this book because it would have not been possible without you. I LOVE YOU DAD…

ACKNOWLEDGMENTS

Coach Jacobs: You taught and modeled leadership before I ever knew what the word truly meant. You are the greatest role model of structure and discipline. Thank You! Big Love…

Coach Tarver: Your strength through your trauma modeled how a man is a father and husband. You are a giver in life. Only Love…

Coach Reeves: You told me, "Once you quit once, you will quit the rest of your life." That quote motivated me to never quit in the game of life. Only Respect…

My Big Brother Rudy: You endured two losses that I cannot even conceptualize. You are my hero forever. True Love…

My Big Sister Rosemary: The 2nd greatest woman I have ever met, after Mom. True Love…

Frankie My Blood Brother: You were a true People's Champion. Literally, in the ring and in life. When you walked into the room, time stood still. Your opponents in the ring were in trouble; your friends and clients outside of the ring were truly blessed. You will always be my blood, my heart, and my soul. May you Rest In Peace, my Brutha. I love you forever.

S.T.A.R.: Sharla, Tiffani, Amanda, Richard (me). You three inspire me every day with your beautiful ways! The Universe brought us together forever. Absolute Love…

Tiffani: Your beauty and grace are the universe. Lexy's passing only cemented your courage and vision going forward. You are a messenger in the humanistic realm. True Love…

Melanie: We were in the right place at the right time; you made my life grow. Thank you for three beautiful sons who have hearts of gold. True Love…

Bobby: May you always rest in peace, my brother. You inspired me every day with your creative mind. 44 Forever! My true Dawg for eternity! True Love…

Drake, Keegan, & Kaleb: You guys are my everything – beautiful, graceful, creative, and hearts of gold. Your beauty is limitless. True Love…

Dante: Truly one of the most gifted people I have ever known. From National Champion to a beautiful person. Your soul is the universe…I love you.

Sandy: I am so proud of how you have handled your loss. Your family is my family; we are brothers forever. Thank you for letting me in…so beautiful! True Love…

Ryan H.: Brother, you are an example of how a pro football player can also be compassionate, kind, open, and vulnerable. Bless you, Bro. Big Love…

Danny: You are the wind beneath my wings. You were my first role model, rugged and graceful. I can't thank you enough for your beauty. I live and love for you. True Love…

Lexy: April 25th 2019 changed me forever. It made me see Tiffani in a new way. It crystalized her beauty and grace beyond me. Please guide us. True Love…

Scotty H.: You were vulnerable before it was in vogue to be such; you are a true example of how to live to love. True Love…

Tammy: You allowed me to be Rikki when coaching me, a brilliant insight and application. Now you are my coach forever! Absolute Love…

T.J. Cunningham: You connected with kids like no other. I am so proud of how you became the true educator you were meant to be. Rest in peace, my brother. True Love…

D-Lo: You know me as well as any male walking this earth. You have been there for me through the fire and beyond. We are beyond family; we are blood. True Love…

Julius T.: I will never forget our version of the Friday afternoon club; 1:00 p.m., every week. You grew me in ways that fortify me to this day. Can't wait to call you Doctor T!

TABLE OF CONTENTS

FOREWORD

Doctor Rick Perea is an amazing man with whom I have been fortunate to spend so much time. He was committed to being there for me and teaching me, not just what it means to understand therapy but what it means to be a human being. Is he a scholar, professional athlete, and world champion performance psychologist, yes, but his passion and true commitment to others goes beyond his professional endeavors.

For me to explain his intentions and commitment to people in a few short words is difficult to express; I believe it must be experienced. His laughter, his empathy, and his caring are a unique juxtaposition against his background as an NFL linebacker. A man tasked with delivering "hits" (as a linebacker), is now the man who loves helping people heal from the personal and professional "hits" they may endure in life. His experiences throughout his life and his journey through sports enabled him to develop into the man he is today. His own personal cultural background and richness is something he continually utilizes to connect with others. His diverse lived experiences, from the reservation with his cousins to the MLB clubhouse, have created his ability to listen and empathize with others across cultures, genders, and diverse backgrounds. I personally believe it is these traits that enable him to understand the lived experiences of people from various cultures with whom he interacts and allows him to reach his clients from all backgrounds and beliefs.

I met Dr. P in the spring of 2016. I was excited to meet him because I'd heard so much about him from several of my teammates who I respect on the Denver Broncos. They were all successful and had been able to perform at the top of their respective careers. Each one of them expressed their gratitude and their respect for how Dr. P has helped them along their own personal and professional journeys. Dr. P immediately stood out to me from other psychologists, not because of his vibrant charisma, which he has in abundance, but because of his heart. I can still remember how we spoke at length about how important it is to focus on the inner spirit of the athlete just as much as we focus on the statistics and talking for hours about how important it was to love other people and create an inner environment of well-being. Over time these continued interactions showed me who he was and what is important to him. I can still remember to this day some of those words Dr. P told me, "I want to expand, I want to grow, I want to commit myself to helping more people than I can in my private practice. I want to write and provide a more culturally diverse perspective to the literature of psychology that is not currently communicating a diverse perspective." It's well known that the majority of psychologists and written works in psychology lack insight from people of different backgrounds. Not just ethnically, but from different life experiences outside of the more typical Euro-American culture, I believe there is much more that needs to be described. It is my pleasure to introduce you to Doctor P, my friend and trusted advisor, who propelled me to seek to have my own impact in the space of psychology and performance, helping me to remember that performance is more than just achieving the goal that you've set out for yourself. It is about being in a place of wellness so that, when you reach your desired goal, you will be able to enjoy it. Doctor P is a champion, a father, a survivor, a carer, and a man who draws on unique personal experiences as well as rigorous academic training to help clients and friends enjoy more fulfilling lives. Doctor P's strengths begin with his authenticity and fully show up with his ability to connect with all people. I've had the privilege to see him work with young high school athletes, business professionals, and professional athletes. This isn't what makes Dr. P unique; what makes Doctor P unique is the openness of his heart and his desire to give each one of those of individuals the best of what he has.

Unfortunately, I do not have the time to fully paint the picture of what spending time with Dr. P is like, but if you read through the pages of this book with an open heart and mind, I am convinced you will get to see how spending time with him has helped me grow. I personally want you to know that purchasing this book was the right decision. Dr. P's unique winning perspective is sure to shape not just your ability to perform but your schemas for life as well. I can say this confidently because I have experienced the change myself.

—Julius Thomas, Psy. D. Candidate
All Pro Football Player
Denver Broncos, Jacksonville Jaguars, and Miami Dolphins

INTRODUCTION

In a word, I am passionate. I love, care, and enjoy communicating with people, one-on-one, one-to-many, on radio or TV. I love educating and stimulating thoughts, feelings, moods, and essentially, behavior. I choose to show up fully alive, fully engaged, and fully leading. In one, life-changing moment of my life, I had a decision to make, either to forge forward through the fiery furnace of fear or to retreat as a victim.

We all have those moments of decision when, in an instant, a split second, a moment of time, we must make a decision that will forever impact our lives. That moment is the Decision Point. That moment is the moment leaders are born.

I want to prepare you for that moment. Some of you have already faced that moment, or a mountain of moments, and continue to bear the weight of those events and the follow-on decisions daily. We see the world through a lens that has been altered, skewed, or injured by life. How we respond to that altered or injured state is key to our future healing, quality of life, how we show up in this world, and success as a leader.

I want to share life stories of true experiences with vulnerability and raw emotion. With every story, I hope to offer insight into life-defining moments, to pick through the buried pain and give you tools to catapult you into the leader you were born to become. Leaders are both born into this life and forged through the fires of experience. I want to offer a playbook of sorts, insight, inspiration, the psychology behind the events and the pain; and, the mindset of leaders and champions who have faced similar tragedies and lived to champion their lives.

Life often throws us curveballs, shutouts, fumbles, and opportunities. Murder, suicide, cancer, life-altering, heart-wrenching stories are all part of my life story; I go deep and reveal the pain and the beauty of each event that has shaped my life and show you how, not in spite of these events, but because of these events, I was forged through the fire of life to become a leader.

I share how my experience with murder at only 7 years old served as a catalyst for my life's opportunities (Super Bowl win) and impacted the way I love and lead. I also share how people I know have taken tragedy and transformed the experiences into life's greatest opportunities and joys, which has been the catalyst to cultivate lives of achievement and winning for them. Collectively, we have seen how loss can be a golden opportunity that will launch you and inspire you to live a life at 212°.

Understanding the psychology of leadership, the delivery of communication, and the power in showing up authentically every day will supercharge your life and catapult you into a great leader. Every day is full of decisions, but truly we only have to make one positive decision every day. Join me as I share what that one decision is that will change your life. You were born to lead; now prepare to lead with love and be set free from the pain of your past. It's up to you; this is your moment of decision – your Decision Point.

Dr. P's Leadership Principles to Live By

Get a Check Up from the Neck Up

Decide to Live Life at 212°

Balance Leadership with Followership

Choose Your S.T.A.R. Circle of Friendship

A Leader to All: Gender and Culturally Responsive

Listen While You Lead

Leaders Love Deeply

Embrace Every Loss & Tragedy in the Moment & Beyond

How Loss and Tragedy are Disguises for Opportunity & Growth

Be Silly & Foolish

Lead with Passion

It's Your Life-Altering, Life-Changing,
Destiny-Deciding Moment.
What Will You Decide?

Chapter One

WHEN MURDER KNOCKS ON YOUR DOOR

One Saturday morning, young, 7-year-old Rikki Perea was watching morning cartoons in his Hot Wheels flannel pajamas, and in the next moment, his life would be forever changed, his childhood innocence stolen. The doorbell of his family home chimed, jolting him alert and removing his attention from the animated cartoons on the screen. His parents were in the kitchen, cleaning up from the morning's pancake breakfast. He answered the door to his family's home and there, staring back at him like looming giants, were two uniformed police officers. The taller of the two, looming like a ten-foot giant, locked eyes with him and asked, "Hey, little man. Are your parents home?"

Young Rikki was facing that moment where all true decisions are made, that moment when the terrifying news he was about to hear would forever change the trajectory of his life, and in that small sliver of time, he would have to decide how to respond to this unwelcome news and how it would affect him for his entire lifetime.

With terror gripping his chest and eyes as wide as saucers, Rikki left the door ajar and the giants standing in the doorway as he sprinted as fast as he could to summon his parents to the door, where they would soon hear those nonretractable words regarding the life of Rikki's older brother, Danny.

In that moment, before he ever left the front door's entryway, Rikki's life had changed; decisions beyond his control, enacted by an adult, would forever impact his life, his achievements, and his purpose, and would launch him into becoming a world class champion for life.

"Mom! Dad!" Rikki shouted into the kitchen before his feet ever hit the floor. "Come quick! Something has happened, I just know it," Rikki shouted, wild-eyed and breathing rapidly. His mother was first to the door, wringing the kitchen towel and still smelling like maple syrup, but his dad was only a half-step behind and stepped around her as protector, facing the police officers square in the face. He was a titan of a man, and the news he was about to hear would rip him to his core.

With dread, he asked the inevitable, "Officers? What is it? Is it my Danny?"

From that moment on, life has forever changed for me and for my family. Our "Danny Boy" was gone, just like that. One moment he was part of our very fabric; he was my wrestling buddy, my tug-o'-war and tumble through the house partner, my go-to for so many things, and the brother I looked up to for confidence, direction and aspiration. He was the parochial school champion boxer. He was a fighter, period. He had more grit and determination to win at life than anyone else I knew. How could he be gone forever?

It was so hard to process. My mom, she just kept saying, "Don't you worry about me. I can handle this." But in our family, there was a big, gaping, silent hole. I just had to accept it. I had to go on. I had to deal with it in silence. Alone. Alone is a very lonely and silent place. All that emotion started brewing and stirring inside of me. I found myself brooding in front of endless hours of television, but I never really saw the cartoons anymore. Without a doubt, my childhood was robbed the day my brother was murdered.

Silently, as I processed the pain without truly knowing or understanding what was happening on a humanistic level, I crossed a bridge. A fire began to burn inside of me.

Why me? I thought, *Why my family? What right did someone else have to murder my brother and to leave me without him? To rob my family of this beautiful soul? To rob the world of our deep, courageous and high-spirited Danny?*

That is when I realized my world had changed and everything about my life going forward would too. That's when I realized there was a seed of determination planted in me that would impact how I showed up on the field, in my life, and as a son in my family; that moment I decided I would live life fully, furiously, devoted to purpose and love, to bring joy to my family, and to give them a reason to celebrate our family, in spite of our loss. This event fueled me to victory. Maybe I couldn't control the loss of my brother, but I could control the outcome of my life and how I showed up from this day forward, and I could allow his spirit to live through me, to help me bring about a sweet victory for my family.

Faced with trauma and tragedy, I know we have only one response: to champion the moment and choose to live life at 212°, which is the boiling point of water – a life boiling over with achievement, fullness, love, and victory. In that moment between opening the door to the police officers and turning to run to the kitchen to get my parents, I was running through the years of childhood at a rapid pace and stepping in to the leader I would become by choosing to make Danny's life count and deciding that, from that moment on, no one would ever make me feel like that again or rob me of anything, that I would live life one step ahead of the tragedy and trauma, of the change and thievery that I faced that day. That day, the leader in me awoke, a sleeping giant that would have eventually evolved but could only surface after facing the terror of that day, in that moment.

It is really challenging to conceptualize or verbalize what it feels like to lose your brother when you're seven years old. As a world class performance psychologist, I now have the benefit of an academic and professional career that helps me understand what I experienced that day and how I can use that to help others when faced with life-changing tragedy or stress-inducing performance anxiety from world championships, or even the dynamics of high-stress business or life events.

The brain is not fully developed in a young child, not even close, so for someone so young to begin to understand it from a scientific or anatomic perspective is very difficult. To conceptualize it from an emotional or psychological view, however, will lead to a better understanding and get to the root of the reason behind the associated negative emotions or behaviors. I can remember little things like looking at my brother as he lay in the casket, and I'll never forget that smell that death brings. It was a masked, dark, provoking smell that was no longer reminiscent of the freshly showered athlete I knew. What I know now to have been the embalming fluid or substances used to prepare his body was the very fragrance that I would recall time after time, and that would lead me to dig in deeper. At that time, I wondered what the heavy smell was, and now, I'll smell that smell forever. In that moment, nothing made sense as I tried to process it.

Why was my brother laying in that casket? How did that happen? Oh, that smell. What is that smell?

THE MOMENT LEADERS ARE BORN

I looked at his hair and saw how it was so carefully groomed, how he looked so peaceful, and how his nose still had a bump on it from boxing just a few weeks before he was murdered. I'll never forget every detail because at seven years old, I had a unique vantage point. I was about as tall as the casket, so I was at eye level and peering straight in over his chest, taking it all in. I think that really brought me close to the experience and, at an intimate level, helped me understand that he was no longer alive.

My brother, a sturdy, sculpted boxing champion, the epitome of strength and a true warrior, was no longer here on this earth. It was a devastating blow. My mind was already beginning to be wired to think like a champion, to use this experience as fuel to launch me from loss to future wins so that his life and legacy would live on. His death fuels me every day to keep giving, loving, doing, and serving more. I love you, Danny, my brother forever.

Since becoming a psychologist and with the beauty of time, which helped to heal the pain to a tolerable point, I know now that my synapses, my presynaptic and postsynaptic terminals, were altered.

Presynaptic is relating to the nerve cell that releases a transmitter substance into a synapse during transmission of an impulse. In transmission, the postsynaptic membrane receives a signal from the presynaptic cell and responds appropriately. Basically, one pathway sends information and the other receives the information, and in the exchange, we process the information and then determine how to respond to it.

From that experience at such an early age in my childhood development, neural pathways were really altered (neuroplasticity), and they impacted (neurogenesis) the way that I looked at people, life, and friendship. I wasn't sure who I could trust. I wasn't letting my emotional walls down anymore. I was determined to come out a fighter, one step ahead of the enemy and the ones who could steal my joy and make me feel like that ever again.

In the early years, you trust everyone; you take them at face value – they are friends of the family, neighbors, part of your community. You let your guard down and you genuinely let them inside your circle, your safe zone, your family. You grow up loving and trusting everyone in that circle.

Then, I learned the dark, ugly truth: It was Danny's best friend who stabbed and killed him, all out of jealousy. The influence of alcohol was probably a factor in the moment, but more importantly, I would learn, as a way to eradicate anxiety on his part.

What I learned while becoming a psychologist is that when the brain is changed from murder, from loss, from losing someone that you looked up to, it's a structural change to the brain and all that is under development (the prefrontal cortex does not stop developing until approximately 24.5 years of age).

It's really something that you can't even explain as it manifests itself over the years, and the impact is pervasive to every area of life. I might not have known this then, at that moment in the funeral home, but I do know one thing was very clear to me as I stood by my brother's casket: I was now different.

Not long after his funeral was over, I knew a decision had to be made. At first, I would walk into his room and see his bed fully made; it hadn't been slept in and nothing was out of place. It was eerie, unsettling, and provoking me to angst. But I kept going back into that room. I kept going back in there, thinking that I would find his bed unmade, that maybe I hadn't understood what had happened. It didn't seem real or possible, but every time, every day, it grew more and more real and more and more difficult to walk past his bedroom because I knew he wasn't coming back, *ever*.

THE MOMENT LEADERS ARE BORN

And then it happened, that moment that I knew I had to decide. I had to be strong for my mom. In the night, I could hear her weeping and crying herself to sleep. She never told us and never cried in front of us, but I could hear her at night. I remember wanting so desperately to do something, anything, thinking, *How can I stop that? How can I stop her from feeling that pain? What can I do?*

And even at seven and a half years old, I knew I could do something. I decided that I had to be really grown-up and strong. I had to help my mom overcome this pain. I had to be the difference-maker in the face of this tragedy. I learned that this was more than possible and that I could.

I'd wake up in the morning, and the first thing I'd do is hug my mom and comfort her the best that I could as her young son and say, "You okay, Mom? How are you?"

Every time she would say, "I'm good, Son. Don't you worry about me. I'm good. I can handle this. I don't want you to worry about me."

Even in her pain, she was worried about me and everyone else. But I did worry about her and strived to be the best son I could to help fill the void Danny left, because I knew how much she loved Danny. In fact, it was so apparent how much she loved him, she left a love note for the world to see. She had engraved on his headstone, "Our Danny Boy."

"Our Danny Boy." She didn't just call him Danny, he was our "Danny Boy" – such an affectionate way to address her son. This was the kind of mom she was, she loved fully. And this was the kind of love Danny evoked from others, as well.

Danny was an incredible human being for his 18 short years in this life. He was tall, handsome, and an fierce fighter. In fact, he had just won the Golden Gloves Championship before he was killed. One of my most treasured pictures is of my father, Danny, and my brother Rudy, and you can see the tape on Danny's nose taped from a recent boxing match nick. That was a calm match, in comparison, and a minor injury, to say the least. Mostly, I just recall him as an incredible human being. The things I remember are when he used to babysit me sometimes and I'd be riding my Big Wheel or maybe my trike down the street, and if I got too far down the street, I'd hear his recognizable whistle calling me to return closer to home. He'd whistle, and that was my signal to turn around and come back. Sometimes I'd push the limits by going a little bit further, to test the boundaries, but he would always come get me, and he'd say, "Come on, Man. Let's go." And I can remember at seven years old saying, "I'm not a man, I'm a boy." And he said, "All right, boy. Let's go."

He was always careful to look out for me, and he treated me with respect.

We shared a lot during those times he watched over me. He was my big brother, and I was his baby brother, but he treated me like I was cool; it wasn't a burden for him to watch me. He always made it seem like it was no big deal, we were having fun together. I remember another time of him wrestling with me. I'll never forget this because it showed me how emotional our family was and how much we shared feelings with each other. One day while Danny was babysitting me, we were wrestling on the front lawn. He was 18 at the time, a well-conditioned athlete, and I might have been scrappy and ready to go toe-to-toe with him, but I was still just seven years old. We were wrestling, messing around the way brothers do, and I can remember it hurting sometimes from his intent to conquer. You know, maybe I got nicked up a little bit, but no big deal. We were just messing around. But this one time, it was a little more serious. Later that night my mom was giving me a bath in the bathtub. I can remember her grabbing my wrist and raising my hand above my head to clean under my arm, I screamed with an incredibly loud screech. She said, "Rikki, what's wrong?" I winced and grunted a little, "Oh, Mom, my shoulder hurts. Oh no. I don't know, just a really sharp pain."

She went and told my dad, and my dad said, "There's probably something wrong with it. We should take him in." They took me to the doctor the next day, and sure enough, I had a fractured clavicle. My arm was put in a sling. I was told to take it easy and was sent home. To this day I will never ever forget as we got out of the car and we walked up the driveway, and Danny came out the front door. He looked at me, and he's like, "Bro, what's wrong with your shoulder?"

My mom looked at him and with a really stern voice she said, "You did this! You broke his collar bone wrestling." Her disapproval was obvious.

My dad quickly responded, "Annie, honey, settle down. He didn't mean to do it."

My mom was quick to my defense, "You need to understand how strong you are Danny."

She was fiery mad and wanted him to understand the difference in our ages and his strength.

I bravely thrust out my chin and tried to play it down, "Don't worry, Man. You didn't mean to do this. You didn't mean to break my collar bone. I know you didn't. We were having fun, Bro." Then I remember Danny kneeling down on one knee, looking me in the eye as he said, "Man, Bro, I am so sorry. I'd never, never do anything to intentionally hurt you. You know that."

"I do," I said, looking up at him, "I do, Man. It's good. Don't worry about it, Man. I'll be ready to go in a week or so. We'll do it again, Man." And so that was one of the memories that stood out for me of how sensitive and caring he was, about how much I looked up to him, because I could see the tears welling up in his eyes, of his true sorrow that he had hurt his little brother. It was all in fun, but he would never hurt me; he truly looked after me and loved me.

Another great memory is captured in a favorite photo where I'm standing up in my crib and Danny has a boxing glove on his hand, holding it up to my face like he's punching me. So funny, you know, just something boys would do.

I have another older brother, too. Rudy. I've got to tell you, the moment I could walk, my brothers were teaching me how to box and how to defend myself. They were proud to have a younger brother, and they included me in everything. Even in my crib they were teaching me how to fight back, how to box, how to be a champion. It really molded me to be tough but not closed to my emotions. My brothers showed me love and tight brotherhood; they valued our family and me as their little brother.

I saw my brothers be very emotional, loving, sensitive, and caring. I witnessed my mom, who was very empathic. She was always touching us, running her fingers through our hair, caressing us, showing us love through physical touch, hugs, and gestures. My dad was a very strong man who rarely showed emotion except at certain times in his life. I am sure that was from his family background and how he was brought up. He was raised on a farm in an area of southern Colorado called the San Luis Valley. People who were raised down there were rocks, pillars, amazingly hard workers and resilient people. My dad was forced to quit school in the third grade because his dad wanted him to help on the farm. My dad, Rudy Sr., was able to carve out a beautiful life by teaching himself algebra, among other academically oriented topics. But my mom showed me love in real ways, and my brothers did too through our close relationships and childhood experiences. My experience with Danny, his murder, his absence, facing the loss of my bigger brother, really influenced my life. It left a hole but fuels me to love more and work harder in life.

I'll never forget the day when the police officer knocked on our door. I can remember it was a very sunny day. I remember the contrast of having a sunny day and the dark news that would follow. The only other thing I remember about that is them asking my parents for Danny's full name, and then one of them saying, "Your son's been hurt, and I think you better follow us to the hospital." I didn't know "hurt" would mean dead and gone forever. "Hurt" was when Danny accidentally broke my collar bone wrestling with me. I would later learn that Danny would be mortally injured, killed by his good friend, someone he trusted.

We all piled into the car, not knowing for sure what the outcome would be. At least, I didn't. Coincidentally, my brother Rudy, 21 years old at the time, lived two blocks away from the hospital that Danny had been taken to. As we drove through the streets, I wondered how Danny had been hurt. Had he been hurt in some kind of motorcycle accident or car accident? I really didn't know. We went straight to my brother's house. I remember my sister Rosemary, my mom, and I went into my brother's house. His wife at the time, Sandra, was there. We all walked into the house and sat on the living room couch. Then only my brother and my dad took the two-block walk over to the hospital to learn more about Danny. Looking back on it now, perhaps they knew more than they told us at that time. I went outside to pass the time and was playing in Rudy's front yard, and after what seemed like two hours had passed, they came back. They weren't smiling, but they weren't emotional either. They walked in the house, and I remember running up to my brother Rudy and saying, "Hey, Man. How's Danny? How's Danny?"

Not even looking at me, he said, "Come in the house."

Confused, I followed closely behind him, and as we walked into the house, I remember Rudy saying, "He didn't make it. He didn't make it."

I remember the emotional wails, the deep, loud wailing and crying from my mom and then from me because, more than anything, I didn't understand anything that was going on, but I could see the look on my Dad's and Rudy's faces, and I could see my mom crying. I was like, "What do you mean? What do you mean he didn't make it? He didn't make it to the hospital? Or what do you mean?"

I remember my dad grabbing me by the shoulders and saying, "Son, you need to stop crying and settle down a little bit."

"No!" I shouted back, my head swirling and still unsure what reality was at this point. "No. I want to know what happened to Danny."

At that point, my mom grabbed me by the hand and took me and gave me a big hug. I felt her warm tears against my cheek, and I still didn't know at that time that he was actually gone. It was all so confusing and surreal. As people began to gather at Rudy's house, I noticed everybody was crying. Then his girlfriend, Doedee, knocked on the door, and I don't think she had been told, because she had a smile on her face when she came over. Rudy approached her and quietly shared the news; her smile was immediately gone, and she joined my mom on the couch in tears.

That scene, that bizarre scene, on a sunny day, where all my family were gathered in my brother Rudy's house, where tears and wailing and crying could be heard, that was the day that I recognized the change in me.

At that moment, seeing all my family, watching his girlfriend process the news, I had to make a decision to support my family and to understand that my brother Danny was actually gone – he was dead.

I didn't understand what had transpired or why no one was talking about the details of what happened, what had led to his death. All we knew was that he had been surprised in an attack where he couldn't defend himself. I am sure everyone was still in shock, gathering the details and trying to process it all, too. But at the time, it made it harder to understand.

As the story that was shared with us goes, Danny, a tall, well-conditioned athlete, a boxer, was with his girlfriend, Doedee, at a party and decided that they were going to leave. His girlfriend's friend approached them and asked, "Can I catch a ride with you?" Danny said, "Sure."

Danny's best friend, George, was also at the party and didn't like that his girlfriend had asked Danny for a ride; he thought Danny was offering her a ride, and perhaps more. I'm not sure what he could have been thinking, but somehow George interpreted the situation as very assertive, I guess, because he thought Danny was flirting with her in some way. That's when George said to Danny, "Hey, before you leave can you come outside? I want to talk to you for a second." Danny said, "Okay, yeah," and told his girlfriend, "I'll be back in a second." George walked ahead of him several steps. As soon as they got outside, he lunged at Danny and stabbed him with a knife. Danny, being the athletic boxing champion that he was, was able to, at the last moment, try and defend himself, but it was too late. He had been mortally wounded.

As the story has it, George, after assaulting my brother in his fit of jealousy, apparently came to his senses and attempted to revive my brother. Because of that effort, he was only prosecuted with manslaughter, not first- or second-degree murder. But because my brother was murdered and left us so abruptly, his life and the representation of his life and of our relationship kept showing up in my life. For example, any time that I saw violent movies or violent shows on TV, I quickly walked away; I never wanted to watch them because they reminded me of what I could only imagine possibly happened to Danny. It was a violent way to die, to be stabbed. I wondered about that often as I grew up. What did that feel like for Danny? Not only physically, but emotionally. I just picture him lying on the ground, holding his wound, fatally wounded and wondering what was happening to him. What was he thinking about in those moments, those last moments of his life? Did he think about Mom? Dad? Oh, I'm sure he did. Our sister Rosemary, brother Rudy? Oh, I'm sure he did. Me? I hope he did, because that's the painful part – I wasn't there to help him. I wasn't there to save him. I wasn't there to protect him. That was my brother, Man. No one had the right to take him from us.

That would become my mantra and my motivation throughout my life. I couldn't be there for him, but you know what? I could decide. I could decide that for the rest of my life, I'm going to show up in a big way, and I'm going to show up in a way that is unmistakable and impacts the world in a big way.

I had to move on, and life continued to cycle, but it was part of the fabric of who I was becoming. His murder continued to influence my life. I was so empathetic of other people's pain, even at the ages of 10, 12, 13, and every year thereafter; it became part of me. I was so caring of other people, but if somebody threatened me or someone I loved, I was so quick, so quick to protect them. I was fierce. I was fierce because I just didn't want anyone else to ever have to go through what I can only imagine my brother went through.

THE MOMENT LEADERS ARE BORN

So, because of the fact that he was murdered and didn't die of cancer or of polio like my older sister Barbara had years before, his murder, his death, really kept showing up and really influenced my brain and how I forever processed trauma, how I thought about life, relationships, and my achievements going forward. I mean, trauma can really, really alter the neuro transmissions of the brain, and it's apparent that it did for me because I continually thought of that pain and that day and how his life must have ended. His life and his soul live on inside of me forever. That experience and him, they will forever be a part of my life.

I've often wondered why I'm so motivated and so driven in my life as an athlete. Others have noticed and asked, and my response is always, "I live for two," because Danny lives within me. He truly does. His energy, his passion, his smile. It all lives within me. And to this day, I understand how murder has influenced me as a performer in my life, in my relationships, my education, and my career. Trauma and tragedy build the brain and shape your life. My brain was altered that day – my life, my future, and every decision I made going forward from this experience of losing my brother.

Through my education, I later learned that my brain was altered because trauma changes neurotransmission in the brain and how you think; the neural pathways are altered by any perception of trauma and pain. And that becomes a norm, a schema. In the brain, schemas organize information. You could talk to a kid that's never been around murder before about murder, and his/her thoughts would go in a particular direction without any basis for processing the event. But if you mentioned the word *murder* to me, the person who has experienced murder, the thoughts go in a different direction, a personal direction, skewed by the experiences of reality, creating a unique paradigm. The brain begins to crystallize those thoughts, feelings, and perceptions around that pain. There becomes a new normal, and that new normal is altered neurotransmission.

The presynaptic and postsynaptic terminals that we talked about earlier, they operate like a lock and key and have a unique fit. What used to be the key with a perfect fit with a lock, perhaps the postsynaptic terminal, is now blocked, and there's no longer a good fit. So, if you think of a memory of a trauma in this way, that thought must travel somewhere, and when that thought travels in a different manner than the intended original fit, it alters the way we think. There's research to show that, for small children that have been exposed to murder, that murder becomes a norm, more of a norm for them than children who have not experienced that. So, as I grew into adolescence, I realized that I was a very emotional young person. And those emotions oftentimes would interrupt play, interrupt sports, and interrupt performance in some way.

I was able to still be a very good student, and I would eventually become a very good athlete and play football at a championship level, but around the ages of 12 and 13 years, I did really struggle. I struggled with deep emotional pain, and there were times that I wanted to escape from this pain, but I didn't know how. Back in these days, there really wasn't therapy offered, and certainly in our family that was not an option. Not because my parents didn't want us to have it. I don't think they were aware that it was something which was available or good or necessary, or that it was even an option.

I think that's an important piece, that as I went into early adolescence and middle adolescence, I had not received the emotional and mental health services or support that I probably needed. I continued to live on and learn through my educational experiences and through my athletic experiences, expressing myself through physical exertion and my determination to excel. This trauma and my lingering pain, from where it had infiltrated my thinking, showed up as a pattern, and this became evident in my first year of playing youth football.

I "played up" a year, which meant that I played with a group that was one year older than I was. I had only been playing football in the street, at school, on the playground, and stuff like that, but never in an organized setting, where you had shoulder pads and helmets on. This was the first time I'd ever played, but it really came pretty natural to me. The aggression that was required to play football, to tackle people, to block people, to really throw your body and hurl your body at other human beings, actually came quite natural to me too. And looking back on it now, one of the major reasons was that I had a lot of pain inside, unresolved pain from my brother's murder, and this was inside of me, buried. We would often do a drill called the "Mini-Oklahoma Drill" where, as a player, you would lie down on your back, coach would blow a whistle, and the football would be right in the middle of two athletes. You'd get up as quickly as you could and run at each other like two battering rams, attempting to get to the football first.

Oftentimes one of the players ran the football and the other one tackled, and it was just "mano a mano," full-speed contact. Remember, I was playing up a year at this time. I was younger than everybody, and I was actually two years younger because I was a year young for my grade though I was large in stature. My mom started me in kindergarten at four years of age. So, I was actually two years younger than all the rest of my teammates.

Yet, even with the age disadvantage, I was still able to physically dominate because, looking back now, I had an emotional and psychological edge that probably gave me an advantage on the field.

DECISION POINT

See, I would never ever allow anybody to hurt me like someone had hurt and killed my brother. That burned in me in drills, in games, on the field, in life.

That's what I feel builds the brains of champions who have faced trauma and tragedy and loss. That's how murder forges a champion for life. In everything I do, I know deep inside of me, I must be a champion and excel, whatever the standard is.

I can't allow a moment like that to ever face me at the door again. I have to be one step ahead of every potential danger or threat. I must champion every moment and dedicate myself to a life of more. I have to win. I work hard, and I give everything I have because I don't ever, ever want to be in the position that my brother was placed in during one misstep, in one surprise attack. That will always be my perception, that he was helpless and that somebody just took his life and robbed him of every advantage.

As a seven-year-old youth and beyond, I was impacted by the emotionality of murder, the psychology of murder, and the physicality of murder. Fundamentally and psychologically, I was living a fear-based life; great for winning in most contexts, but at what cost? I was not really in touch with my true feelings. The pain was fuel; but the fuel was external. I, in reality needed internal fuel, self-love. There was a lot of pain associated with my performance at this time, but I would later learn to turn that pain into positive change and impact, molding the brain and the mind of a champion by making a higher choice – self-love, a decision to lead, a decision to be more in all areas of my life, to be a champion in sports, a champion in business, a champion in academics, and a champion in life. This I do to impact the world, to honor Danny, and to inspire others to lead in the face of trauma and tragedy and to decide in the moment to be champions of life.

Chapter Two

THE MINDSET OF A CHAMPION

Though I found a physical and emotional outlet for my pain through football, it became a pattern for me; I always had something to prove. My brother was taken unfairly. My brother was really just the etiology of a life of compensation. I just kept playing the thoughts and the events of his murder over and over again in my mind. All the way through middle school and high school, the pain kept getting pushed down, but the thoughts in my mind and my spirit were on a constant loop; it fueled me, not necessarily in a positive way, to push harder and to be more. It was my way of dealing with the pain.

It was a representation of my life that I needed to, at all times, make sure that no one around me in my ecosystem or my family was ever hurt again, much less killed.

For me it became really important to prove that I was strong and that I was there as their protector and to make things better; this became a time of proving a lot in my life – academically, athletically, and even socially.

By tenth grade, my football career was off to a really good start. I was "starting" on our sophomore team. I focused and channeled all my energy into the game. I was able to play really well and be successful for the team.

DECISION POINT

Something very important happened to me in tenth grade. I had made a very important decision at this point. I had asked myself, *Am I going to really work to be great, or am I going to decide that football isn't for me because maybe it's too violent?* Then something happened that would make a great impact on me.

One day, we were doing the very familiar, "Oklahoma drill." That's where we line up, one-on-one, with a running back on one side and the person trying to tackle that running back on the other. It was a very competitive environment. All of the players stood around and watched us compete on the field. It was a very, very hypercompetitive environment with players yelling and cheering us on. Even though I was a year, sometimes two years younger than my teammates, I was considered to be one of the better players on the team. I was going against a player that was much bigger than me during this drill. As we lined up for the "Oklahoma drill," our coach blew the whistle, and I went to tackle this player at full throttle. He lowered his shoulder and ran right over me. As we call it today, he "trucked" me. He beat me in a way that there was no mistaking his intention to win at all costs. It more than jarred me.

One thing about sports is that it's the highest level of social comparison. When you take a test or an exam in a class, if you fail that test, there's two people that know it – the instructor and you. But in sports, when you fail, everyone who's watching sees it. *Everyone knows.* It was a very, very embarrassing point for me when I got run over. When I got up, I walked to the back of the line, and I can remember saying to myself and out loud to anyone in ear shot, "That will never, ever happen again."

I could hear my teammates, my friends, with the "oohs" and the "ahhs" at the person who had trucked me, and I repeated to myself, "*That will never ever happen again.*"

That forged my mindset and, I believe on that day, the mindset of a champion. That day when I went home, I told my mom, "Mom, I want to get a weight set for the basement because I want to start working out, not only during football season. I want to work out on my own for myself. I want to get protein powder because I want to get bigger. I want to get stronger. I want to be everything I can be. I want to show up as my best."

From that moment on, I was different. My life changed in terms of the way I approached the game of football and faced big challenges head-on. I began lifting weights every night after football practice. I began drinking protein powder every day. Within a short period of time, I had gained a lot of strength and muscle and would eventually hold the all-time highest bench press record in the history of my high school, which has still never been broken to this day. I had faced my fear and arrived at my decision point. In that loss, that perceived deficit, I launched to a higher version of myself and revealed the champion within me.

That day, with people and other teammates on the sidelines laughing at me, I had to make the decision, *Am I going to allow people to run over me? Am I going to allow people to truck me and beat me in front of everybody, or am I going to respond?*

In the work I do now, we have what's called the "10/90 rule." Life is 10% of what happens and 90% how we respond to it. That was my response that day before I even knew it had a name. That was the day I decided (decision point) *that will never happen again.*

The second thing that happened to me in high school that was a defining point was when one of my best friends, Steve Newell, and I went to a teen dance night event. They had this at a regular dance club normally limited to adults, but it was open for teens only on this particular night. They didn't serve alcohol, they just served soft drinks.

DECISION POINT

I've always loved to dance ever since I was very young, and I think I have a real sense of rhythm, so I love dancing. My friend and I went to have a fun time. Some of the people there we knew, and some of the people that were there we didn't know. It was really a powerful evening because we were enjoying each other's company and what we were doing – just having fun.

I'm in my own world, moving to the music, when all of a sudden Steve taps me on the shoulder and says, "Hey, look over there in the corner. Isn't that Carter Bradley?" Carter Bradley was a grade above us and taking advanced placement courses, so smart and beautiful and senior to us. The reason I know that is because the class we were in together was an advanced placement course, our social studies class. We were in different grades, but this class was open to anyone who qualified for it, regardless of grade level.

It was pretty well-understood that Carter Bradley was the most attractive female in our high school by a long way. She was a model and a competitive dancer, super smart, and a standout in our school. She was basically a unicorn.

I looked over to where she was sitting, surrounded by a lot of people chatting with her as she was laughing and sharing a story with them.

"Yeah, that is her," I said. "Wow, what's she doing here tonight?"

We used to think she only dated guys who were in their 30s or something. It wasn't true, but that's what we thought because she was that beautiful and sophisticated.

We marveled at her being there but headed back to the dance floor with some girls we recognized from our class. We danced for a few songs. Then I was standing there and I felt someone else tap me on my shoulder. I thought it was my friend Steve again. I turned around, still moving to the music, and to my surprise, it was Carter Bradley.

"Aren't you in my social studies class?" she asked coyly.

I said, "Yeah, I am." I couldn't believe she was talking to me.

She said, "Oh, gosh, what are you guys doing here tonight?" referring to me and Steve.

"Oh, we're just here chilling, Man. Just dancing, having a good time." Steve looks at me real cool and everything, equally surprised that she approached us – well, me.

"Oh, okay." She looked right at me and said, "Yeah, I saw you over there before and I thought, 'Wow, okay, I should go over and say hi.' "

"What's your name again?" she asks, seriously looking interested at me.

I said, "Rick." So, we talked for a few minutes while the music was getting louder in the background.

Then she leaned over and whispered in my ear. "You know, you're the only good-looking guy in that whole school," she said.

I was in disbelief because it's one thing to have a girl say that to you, which is a very nice compliment, but it's another thing when a girl says that to you and she's literally the prettiest girl in your whole school. And she came up directly to me and whispered it in my ear!

That was another turning point for me since this older, beautiful supermodel was basically telling me she was attracted to me; I must be something, somebody. We ended up dancing that night, having a good time. She actually gave me a ride home because Steve had long gone before we were done dancing.

But the whole point is that she chose me. She came up to me and literally told me that she thought I was attractive and that I was the most attractive male in the entire school. My head swelled to the size of a globe. You couple that with my football acumen and my athletic performance, and I was well on my way to performing like a champion.

In fact, Carter Bradley taught me a lot. She was extremely

intelligent and used three-, four-, and five-syllable words often. I had not heard of them before, so I truly learned a lot from her. She was very sophisticated, came from an affluent family, from big money. She had a nice car and had a certain understanding of social things, like what to wear to different events. She really understood a lot. As a model, she traveled and was exposed to a high level of competency and acumen in the social realm. I grew in that relationship with Carter Bradley.

Now not only had my athletic competencies been built, but I was elevated on the social level, as well. I mean, when you're known as one of the best football players in your high school and you're dating the prettiest girl in your high school, your social status just naturally elevates. It's kind of the human food chain. I was pretty much at the top, and I was only in eleventh and twelfth grade.

The other thing that Carter brought to the table that was really a launching point for me was that she challenged my perspective on how to turn loss into beauty. She had lost her father and her brother in a plane crash. When she revealed that to me, I told her about my brother who had been murdered. We had this commonality of tragedy and loss, and this became a launching point for our relationship. We spent many days and evenings at the park talking about our losses, about what it felt like the moment we had to hear the news. She had so many questions for me about what it felt like to lose someone to murder. What she and I agreed upon at the end of the day was that we both had experienced loss in a deep and profound way, and that was our bond.

The relationship became so much more than just an attraction or a puppy love in high school. It was based on intellect, emotions, psychology, our shared loss and deep emotional feelings, and it really taught me so much about myself. I learned more about communication skills and compassion for others and really how to comport myself around people within a relationship.

That relationship, and the bond we shared was really a launching point for me and my growth, but also socially. Up to this point I had experienced some success athletically and also some success academically. But I really wasn't applying myself at this point in the way that I could. Who would have guessed, based on my academic performance then, that I would possess a terminal degree, a Ph.D.? That should encourage a lot of people – we aren't defined by our past or our past performance. It is deeply a part of us, but what we do with it (10/90 rule) is what ends up defining us.

We talked about turning loss into beauty and then into leadership. As I said, she traveled as a model, both nationally and internationally, and through this developed as a leader. She learned to communicate with a broad spectrum of people and how to handle herself in many different, sometimes stressful, situations. She would come back, and we would talk at length about her experiences. I learned a lot about people and the world through her.

As my vocabulary began to expand by listening to the words that she used and after the hours we spent communicating, I began to change and grow; my leadership skills began to expand, and soon I was a captain on my football team. I was asked to speak in front of our team and motivate the team. They respected me and what I had to say. Oftentimes, I would talk about loss with the team, not to take things for granted and to really relish the moment, in the day, and we now call that mindfulness.

That experience as a captain and that relationship really crystal-lized my character and formed the leader in me. We learned how to take pain and make choices to turn it into something better. That's where the growth came, and together we learned to turn it into leadership. Life throws you a lot of curveballs. She and I would talk at length about asking why did she have to lose her brother and her dad? That was her most pressing question. Why on that given night did the plane have the difficulties that sent it down? What was the probability of that happening, of both her family members being on board and that happening? Then there was the whole deeper side of how it impacted our psychology, our emotionality, and our functioning skill systems. We were both grateful to have each other to talk about it. What are the chances of even that?

It was through this that I learned how to manage and lead in spite of those trials and tribulations. When I met her and found out about her loss, it made me feel better in the sense that I knew I wasn't alone in experiencing such a profound loss, that somebody else had, and that I could talk about it and share every feeling, thought, and question with someone who understood me. It was very powerful and contributed enormously to my emotional health and leadership development.

Leadership is developed through verbalization, vocalization, and through nonverbal communication. The in-depth conversations that Carter and I had over a period of time really led us to be open and also to develop as dynamic communicators. Her vocabulary was so vast. It expanded mine and helped me develop into a dynamic communicator and speaker with skills that would follow me into my career.

Pain and life experiences add layers of context. When you feel pain and you know pain, it really can influence the way you approach people and connect with people. I think that's a key component of this piece of how to manage and lead through the curveballs of life. In fact, I would say the curveballs of life are really what inspire us to be the most beautiful people, the best versions of ourselves. I know it's helped me come to know and connect with some of the most beautiful people I've ever known. The greatest leaders I have known don't just arbitrarily fall out of the sky, they are forged from the fires and trials of life.

"The most beautiful people in the world we have known are those who have also known defeat, suffering, struggle, and loss and have fought their way out of the depths of despair and the abyss. These people have an understanding of life that fills them with compassion, passion, and a deep loving concern for others as well. Beautiful people do not just happen; they are formed by the life-defining moments of their experiences, and then they *choose* to rise from the ashes and lead with fury, passion, and purpose (author unknown)."

One of the ways that my leadership and communications skills have been utilized as a professional performance psychologist is as a radio and TV expert analyst for local and national outlets. The following is a rendition from one of my radio listeners that became a client at my Performance Facility (ThinkOne) in Denver, Colorado. He chronicles how my communication skills and charisma impacted the delivery of my content. Without a doubt, my relationship with Carter forged my communique, cadence, voice inflection and gestures. David Bovard reveals his interpretation of how he listened to me on the radio first, then how we came together as a dyad/client:

Dr. Rick Perea (Dr. P.) on the Radio with Sandy Clough

The sports appetite is nonstop in Denver, where no matter the time of year, talk radio is always buzzing with the latest Broncos, Nuggets, and Avalanche news. Top of the game is All Pro host Sandy Clough at 104.3 FM "The Fan," where he commands weekday morning prime time. Sandy's connections lead to interviews with local celebrities, including players literally inside the Broncos' huddle. Sandy's style is just the right seasoning of wit, wisdom, and editorial. That's the landscape featuring monthly interviews with Dr. Rick Perea, Sandy's intro to listeners, even though he's known among friends as "Dr. P."

Randomly every few months, listening to 104.3 FM The Fan, I'd catch Dr. P being interviewed. His insights were always a captivating inside sports story, making me more curious with each show. Here's the difference-maker: sports shows are generally full of athletes' interviews about the game and their individual or team challenges, yet it's incredibly rare to hear about any focus on the game from the perspective of the neck up. Many of Dr. P's original sayings kept ringing true for me:

"Championships begin between the ears."

"A winning mind is a calm mind."

"The inside game is knowing when your mind-body is in the Sympathetic or Parasympathetic part of your Autonomic Nervous System." (You can reference the Autonomic Nervous System Chart contained at the end of this Chapter and see the Protocol Leadership Cards, in Chapter Thirteen.)

Timing is everything, and for me, this one time something stood out in a new way. It was early September, the final five weeks of my training for a half Ironman. Knowing something was missing, I turned to some of Dr. P's sayings and began to think them through. Even though I felt physically ready, my training needed icing on the cake, an extra something. In the game from the neck up, I wasn't exactly out of shape, but not quite in championship-shape, either. It was Thursday morning, and once again Sandy, Orlando Franklin, former NFL offensive lineman, and Dr. P were rockin' on the radio as I listened during my workout. They were bantering with more stories and insights, very entertaining. These guys were definitely having fun. As the show wraps up, Sandy throws out the usual tag line, "And that's Doctor Rick Perea of ThinkOne, with offices in the Denver Tech Center."

Somehow it landed differently this time, like an invitation that had to be followed. *Need to put that on the To Do list,* I thought.

Flip forward just a few days and it was Sunday morning at the gym, my usual reps and stretch, challenging cardio, and Ironman tune-up in progress. Race day was October 20th in Arizona, and time was short. Sunday mornings tend to be sparse, not too many guys and gals head to the gym at early hours. I noticed a couple of guys chatting it up, and one of them looked to me like a former pro athlete, still in great shape. Yet no one like that at the gym had the VIP look, wore incredibly classy wrist bracelets, and lingered as if they were at the neighborhood BBQ with the family. I would later learn that Dr. P is the perfect blend of masculinity and charisma that makes you think he is two or three people wrapped in one. So eclectic. Smart, warm, compassionate, emotional, and an amazing communicator and listener. Walking past them both, I noticed his snappy black workout shirt with can't-miss lettering on the back, "ThinkOne: The Behavior Design Specialists." I couldn't believe it; he had to be Dr. Perea. As he wrapped up a conversation, I noticed his son was about to start a workout on one of the nearby machines, and I had to introduce myself, sharing the short version of completely enjoying his comments on the Sandy Clough show.

Right off the bat, Dr. P jumped in to describe ThinkOne's Peak Performance, how it applies not just to athletes, executives, and surgeons, but just as much to first responders, to families, to people in general. He was quite the ambassador as well, offering a tour of his facility later that same week. As usual, the story was just as good as on the radio. Simultaneously, another short story was unfolding on the inside.

DECISION POINT

Have you ever run into someone who was the par excellence version of your own *The Roads Less Traveled*? Picture what that might be like. All of a sudden, they're standing in front of you and the conversation unfolds as if it's been going on for years inside your head, and here it is, unfolding in real life, real time, right in front of you. I was a college Psychology major but later graduated instead with a degree in Marketing Management. I was on the college football team for a few months as a walk-on, then I had to walk off, thanks to grades, though I still love the game. There's more. In high school, I was a professional DJ and news announcer at the local radio station; ditto in college, but I retired early after a short stint of two months. At that age, early morning was not my prime time. Thank goodness I've excelled in other fields, diversity being the blessing there as well. Back to Dr. P, the consummate, hybrid super-blend of a peak-performance professional with a Ph.D. in Psychology and the DNA of an NFL linebacker, talking it up on Denver's top sports radio programs. So, there I was, talking the same language with him. It was surreal.

Later that week, I accepted his offer to tour ThinkOne – what a treat. Every bit as much as expected, it's about a designed mindset of training, more so from the neck up, combined with a reimagination of how our bodies work from the neck down.

I was hooked and committed to whatever Dr. P was offering. At ThinkOne, getting into the Ironman final training phase became a banquet of the best mental energy snacks ever. The coaching experience instantly tailored a winning formula to allow me to achieve peak performance. Throughout all phases of the triathlon swim, bike, and run, I had a secret jet fuel: affirmations repeated silently within, or better yet, shouted out whenever the urge hit. With Dr. P's own experience and that of hundreds of athlete clients and lay people as well, the mental game preparation was so effective that I completed the half Ironman, finishing with a terrific time and achieving the success I was after.

The secret sauce at ThinkOne is the collective wisdom within Dr. P, his client dedication, and blending the science of our physical and mental bodies into the art of peak performance – that's championship coaching. To that, add the savvy of holding the opposites of western science and eastern wisdom as one: *ThinkOne*. The coach appears when the athlete is ready. Be prepared, for it may happen at the most surprising time, like Sunday morning at the gym, over a cup of coffee, like it did for me.

Deep thanks, Dr. P, and to your team at ThinkOne.

Chapter Three

THE PSYCHOLOGY OF A WORLD CHAMPION

Maybe I had thrown the baby out with the bath water. Football was a rollercoaster of opportunity; it was feast or famine. As a player, you were putting your all into a game of force, aggression and performance. As a team, everything was riding on that one game, that one performance, that one moment in time, and you were either champions in the eyes of the fans, or you disappointed a whole lot of people who devoted time and money to come see you show up as your best self.

I lived for the game at this point – beautiful girls, overt accolades, making my family proud, and everything about the game itself; there were a lot of things that made it magnetic for me. All I wanted was my first pro contract. I was waiting for the NFL to draft me, or at least sign me to a free-agent contract. There had already been a lot of talk that it was going to happen. My performance on the field was consistent and solid; I had it in me. It was all I could think about. Then the moment came, and this happened.

Life is full of curveballs, and for me, this was one of them. It was not what I expected. It was not what I sacrificed everything else for, and it certainly wasn't what I dreamed of or thought about nonstop. It was, however, the offer I got. Anyone else might have been doing cartwheels on the sidelines, but for me, it was a blow. I had so much riding on that NFL offer – my family's dreams, too. I didn't want to disappoint them.

It was, after all, a great offer. That loss would launch me into a destiny I couldn't have seen at that time as a high school senior. I thought I would be drafted in the late rounds, but the draft came and went, and I was not drafted by the teams that all but promised me they would, teams like Dallas and Seattle. As such, I had nine teams that wanted me to sign a free agent contract. I wanted to sign with the Raiders, of course. As a defensive player I loved their black-and-silver tradition of playing aggressive football. I listened to their offer but probably made one of the biggest mistakes of my football career: I listened to my mom and adhered to her request. She postulated that I should sign with the Denver Broncos so she and the family could watch me play.

I signed my first pro contract with the Denver Broncos in 1983 as an undrafted free agent linebacker. The offer was sweet, better than many, but it would lead me down a different path than I expected and would have me questioning my future in football. You see, pro football was about one primary thing: money. I quickly realized that decisions were often based on the economics of the game. For example, we had a middle-round draft choice at linebacker that year that had very few football skills. He was an amazing athlete but was not a good football player. Because they had invested a good deal of money in him, they kept him for a few years to see if he would "develop," which never happened. Conversely, players that were not draft choices were given little time to prove themselves before being discarded as has-beens.

That experience was, in many ways, illuminating, showing that pro football was a very different place than what I perceived it to be as a kid growing up. Sometimes your dreams distort the reality of the experience. So, while you are growing towards your dream, remember to keep it real. Think it through and make sure what you're working for is what you think it is and the right thing for you and your future self.

You see, in football there's more than the desire to play; there's a whole psychology of self and life that goes into committing to playing and to winning.

Before considering the psychology of a world champion and what it takes to perform at that level, we have to delve into the science of performance, and that pertains to the autonomic nervous system (see illustration at end of chapter). We have two sides that impact our every move and decision, the sympathetic and parasympathetic sides. Both come into play when we are out on the field giving it our all, or even for the CEO sitting behind a desk, making high-level decisions, and negotiating mergers, acquisitions, and real estate deals with a lot at stake. Even when parents are making in the heat of the moment decisions; guaranteed, if you are making decisions when you are on the parasympathetic side, you will generally make intentional, purposeful well thought out decisions. If you are on the sympathetic side, you will generally just react in frustration and perhaps even anger. Leaving in your wake, flustered and perhaps psychologically injured participants. Whatever your winning goal is, that's your playing field, and the same applies.

As stated earlier, for peak performance, a player – anyone invested in the outcome – must adhere to parasympathetic elements.

You don't need to get too deep or have a love for science, but a basic understanding of our autonomic nervous system helps you understand the many factors at play. You don't have to beat yourself up for wrong decisions, indecisions, or decision-making that's out of left field. It gives you insight into to the many impulses your mind and body are processing simultaneously. When we begin by understanding this, we gain greater insight as to why we made a decision or avoided one.

For example, when I was on the field and there were lot of perceived pressures– family performance, a need to please them and my coaches, and the reality of competing in a hyper-competitive occupation that could literally could end any day, my brain would interpret this climate as a threat. As a result, the pituitary gland would automatically release more adrenaline and thus automatically elevate to the sympathetic side which is where anxiety and stress live. As such, I was basically living a fear-based existence and literally wore myself out being on the sympathetic side, draining my energy physically, emotionally and psychologically. Then one day, I actually "let-up" when tackling a running back and realized I had to seriously rethink what I was doing with my life. This was so uncharacteristic of me. I was fierce, aggressive and loved hitting opposing players. Little did I know at this moment, my challenges were mainly mental, not physical, like a simple analysis might lead me to believe.

Was this the future I wanted to drive hard for? Was this part of my daily dose? Were a few hours of winning worth the trade of my future? At that moment, I just wanted to get rid of the anxiety, get rid of it all. There was more – the constant pressure to perform. I recall being in the locker room and asking where a teammate was and someone would respond, "Ah man, they got cut." Would I be cut like the guy next to me just last week? Could I give it my all and win week after week? Did I want to trade my brain health and my future for this?

I couldn't balance all the charging thoughts or reason them away.

DECISION POINT

My sympathetic side of my autonomic nervous system was working overtime, preventing a resolution. Eventually, I threw the baby out with the bath water and tossed my helmet aside, leaving pro football – perhaps for all the wrong reasons.

I was experiencing high levels of anxiety, exacerbated by the insecurity of the pro football environment, the transient, temporary slot each of us was constantly battling to keep. It was very different than college football, where there was security in your playing position, where you were actually revered. But in pro football, you were only as good as your last performance.

I thought about the constant anxiety a lot and thought maybe it was that I didn't love football anymore, but that wasn't it. I was feeling anxiety around the transient part of football, that one day you're here, the next day you could be gone. I always wondered to myself, *How could this be a place of safety and love when it really isn't?* We all need that peace and security of belonging and safety and acceptance. No one thrives in uncertainty (unless they live a fear-based life), fear of being replaced, and in such volatile environments. In many ways, I feel it was a very healthy thing for me to leave pro football because I didn't want to live a fear-based life. We certainly don't perform as our best selves when we are walking on eggshells and waiting for the hammer to fall. Tough-guy football player or not, all I've ever wanted in my life was safety and love; my brother's murder taught me that.

We certainly didn't have psychologists around the NFL at that time. We just dealt with the mental part of the game on our own. For me that meant I did not deal with it or verbalize it or gain wisdom from any wise mentor. I dealt with my anxiety, induced by the hypercompetitive industry that I was in, by simply quitting. After two years, I just walked away.

THE MOMENT LEADERS ARE BORN

I made the mistake of perceiving my anxiety as a clue that I didn't enjoy football anymore, but it was the environment, the culture, if you will, and I couldn't live with the uncertainty or the physical ramifications anymore. I made the mistake of thinking my anxiety was surrounding football, yet it was more about security in my position and separating that from the game of football itself.

The reality is, I did still love football, but in that moment, head swirling from a recent battering and the intensity of the sport while sitting in a locker room of ghosts of former players, I made a snap decision. I had to choose one side or the other to find my peace and resolution; I could not keep living in the adrenaline mode of fight or flight. One side of the autonomic had to win. Football lost that day.

Later, through my studies for my advanced degrees, I would read case studies that would bring me greater clarity of this earlier decision. I threw my career away just to get rid of that high, intense anxiety, trying to reduce it. I liken it to the analogy of when someone takes their own life – it's a permanent solution for a temporary problem.

If I had had someone like me, a qualified performance psychologist, to talk to about this issue and separate the anxiety from the role, to help me understand where it was really originating from, then I would have been able to better understand and resolve my internal battle. The insecurities, the raw parts of myself, and recognize it as separate from the environment or my position as a football player, and I would have been able to continue on as a football player. This was a light bulb moment for me; it was a very illuminating experience for me to explore all the facets of that important decision and understand what was truly going on.

I couldn't go back to football, at this point. That opportunity was now part of my journey, part of who I was becoming, and part of my former season. However, the transition allowed me the time to go back to school and pursue my education, which allowed me to find a place for who I am at my core and to impact others while still focusing on athletics and professional performance.

Like everything I do, I went full-focus to acquire several graduate degrees over the next eight years, in search of knowledge. It also compensated for the lack of competitiveness I had experienced and enjoyed in pro football. It was the first time that I didn't have football in my life on a competitive level. Academia was a good outlet; it kept my mind in physical, emotional and psychological training daily.

I'm very proud of my education. To be a former football player, to go back to college and acquire a Ph.D., is still one of my greatest achievements to me, personally. It actually makes sports seem small in comparison because, though my ability as a football player was great in the sense that I had speed, athleticism, and the mentality to play linebacker at such a high-performance level, to have a high level of education lifts me up every day in a much different way; it makes me feel different in my own eyes and, I suspect, in the eyes of others. I feel the respect for my accomplishment. Mostly I think this because I came from a family who didn't put an emphasis on formal education. I became inspired after watching my sister study late at night to become an RN, an oncology nurse. In one generation, I helped to shift my family's legacy, and I did that through pro football and through the discipline and achievement of academics. That's why it means so much to me, I think. I did it to give my family hope and bring them joy from the years of pain.

Education helps shape leaders. In the past I wasn't good at academics, and I believed the lie that I wasn't smart enough or good enough. My grades weren't very good in middle school and especially not in high school because I was so distracted with girls and sports – everything was a priority except academics. Once I started seeing results for my efforts in my college classes, I was able to find freedom and satisfaction in my pursuit of greater education and develop more as a leader. It was new to me to excel in something besides physical activities like football. I encourage everyone to pursue higher education if you have ever had a thought to do so; it will challenge your thinking and empower you to go for greater goals. You will begin to think self-love and see yourself as a champion.

I fell in love with psychology and realized it was my calling right from the beginning. There are three levels of occupation in industrial/ organizational psychology, and those are job, career, and calling. A calling is a place where your knowledge, skills, and abilities (KSAs), are keenly matched with what you do.

That's one of the elements of living life and performing at a high level – that your KSAs are matched with your calling, with what you do for a living, with your life in alignment with your natural talents; you are operating in your wheelhouse and you can find deep purpose and satisfaction there as a result.

In this perfect intersection, or nexus, of everything, you are at your core; It is where I call "life at 212°." The expression comes from the known temperature at which water boils and creates live steam – at 212°F. This is like the tipping point, the boiling point.

Live steam is powerful enough to propel a locomotive up a mountain. You see, the difference is that at 211° that locomotive's going nowhere fast. At 212° it's going up the mountain. How many people live their lives at 211°, 210°, 209°, 205°, just a few degrees away from 212°, the temperature where the real action happens, and they don't even realize it? If they would have given the full effort to give that one extra degree, those two degrees more to achieve 212° of effort, output and action, they could be in that train going up the mountain versus sitting at the bottom, making no real progress. That is it, one small degree of difference between optimal performance and mediocre performance.

My assertion is that many people live life not achieving their potential, not being who they're supposed to be, just by one degree. If they understood that small difference, that they're one, two, maybe three degrees of effort away from turning that corner and being everything they're meant to be, then there might be a little extra effort and a lot more high achievers in this society reaching their true potential.

Living life at 212° is a great standard for performance. The beautiful thing is that it is simply a *choice*. It's a daily choice we get to make on how we are going to show up and live our lives. What kind of outcome do you really want? You just have to dig in a little deeper. And you are in complete control of that.

The moment that leaders really catapult themselves above and beyond the average person is that moment when they choose to live life at 212° daily and go all-in, committed to the results they desire. This decision is what separates the pack. Leaders decide daily what type of leader they are going to be and how much they are willing to commit. There is no margin for one degree less. Champions think differently, and they live life fully committed at 212° or higher.

Once you make that decision for 212°, it builds a platform of achieving peak performance with consistency, because you are showing up differently, consistently. When you live life at 212°, you're giving full effort, energy, and attitude. And that's the whole key to living a life at 212°, affecting the three things you can control – effort, energy, and attitude. We call it "EEA." Effort, energy, and attitude are the foundation of peak performance.

All of this plays into the psychology of becoming a world

champion, understanding that if I live life at 212° and give full effort, full energy, full attitude every day, then that's going to catapult me into a different level of performance and achievement, maybe even being a world champion, which I was privileged to attain through football. And it's the exact mindset and psychology that led me to be a psychologist for the Denver Broncos in the 2015–2016 championship season, where consistent 212° performance helped bring home a world championship. I got to be a part of that as a performance psychologist for individual team members, coaches and for the team.

My ability to communicate, to relate and understand players, and to connect with them led me to impactful breakthroughs for individual players who made deciding plays for the win. To bridge my experiences from being on the field as "one of them" to lending insight from my professional position was an ideal intersection of my core self. And then to also connect with them in mind, heart, and professionally was a winning combination. It was an excellent way to bring all these parts of my life together and challenge them to their best performances.

The word *connect* is huge in terms of my work as a psychologist and in being able to interact with people. Connection is done through effective communication and leadership, but the foundation of it is psychology.

Understanding myself and my modus operandi every day allows me to share love, share belief in people, understand others, and to reach and help them through this connection. At the core of this, leaders must know who they are, what experiences they bring to the table, their core values, their choice to perform or not, and how they are going to roll it all in and let it play out.

But the real psychology of a world champion is how to *connect* with people and engage them and challenge them, how to motivate and empower them based on how you show up as a leader – full boil at 212°, acutely aware of your KSAs and how to apply them to your environment and of your EEAs to benefit your position as a leader and your leadership of others. There are psychologists all over the world who have a great knowledge base, but they *don't* know how to connect with people. They don't know how to reach people in a culturally divergent way or how to see the individuality each person brings to the table, being sensitive to leading others for who they are and how they show up in this world, regardless of gender or culture or social background. This is the differentiator and game changer of great leaders. This awareness can profoundly change how you show up as a leader, as a world class champion or not, and how it impacts your world.

KSAs, EEAs, the choice to show up at 212° are equally part of the equation to show up as a high-performing leader in the world. Cultural awareness and divergent thinking come together to form the foundation of psychology on how to show up as a world champion every day.

Let's take a look at the fore-mentioned elements at work to lead on and off the field so that you are challenging yourself to perform at your best. Achieving peak performance is most achievable when we control three very specific things every day: our effort, our energy, and our attitude. Our effort is typically directed at a specific task. How much effort do you give to studying for a specific target activity, such as an exam? How much effort do you give towards preparation for a specific game? How much effort do you give towards a particular presentation in a meeting? When you dig in and deliver your best, you have controlled the effort towards achieving peak performance.

Energy is a little bit different. It's psychological, but it's also that physiological energy we bring to any endeavor; energy can change a room and the outcome of a project or performance of another individual or team. You can do a check of several things that affect your energy to ensure you are performing at your best. Do I bring effort and how is that perceived or received by others? Do I bring a nonverbal effort? Do I use a lot of gestures, and do they serve a purpose to punctuate my communication? Do I use a lot of voice inflection in the way I communicate, or am I not bringing that type of effort? What happens when you just can't muster the energy? Step back and get your thoughts right, do some push-ups or eat a peppermint, change your self-perception, get your mind right, and get your head back in the game. Your desire is for peak performance; to do this, your energy must be high, your thoughts elevated to the possibilities of the outcome. Eat right, skip the caffeine, hydrate, work out the relationship kinks by showing up authentically. When your energy is high, your outcomes are generally great.

Then there's attitude. Attitude is a mindset. It's a purposeful, intentional degree of shaping your thoughts so your thoughts don't shape you; it is impacted by a choice you make and resonates how you show up. If you wake up every morning and allow whatever thoughts that leak into your mind randomly to stay, they can shape you and your day and the outcomes of your day.

Here's an illustration: The average human being has 45,000 thoughts a day, and up to 75% of those thoughts can be self-doubt or negative thoughts – that is up to 33,000 negative thoughts per day that are impacting our mindset and our attitude and that we have the power to change.

If we allow ourselves to be the passive recipient of those thoughts, as many of us do, we live in what we call the proverbial "red box," – the red box is a state of self-doubt and using our words and our postulations in a very negative and self-defeating way, such as, "Well,

I'm not sure I can get that done. I'm not sure I can get this handled." It might turn out to be an okay day, and maybe you can live with those kinds of results.

Then you have the "yellow box." The yellow box is a state of not fully committing to the goal or the outcome; the yellow box is full of doubt, where we say, "Well, I'll give it a try," as if to see what happens, not truly expecting good outcomes. We leave the back door open in case we don't get the desired outcome or achieve what we set out to, leaving the back door as an easy escape route.

Then, there's the "green box," where we want to live. The words, the phrases, the thoughts, and the mindset are all positive – "I can. I will. It's already done. I'm going to do this." You are committed to the goal and you can see the positive outcome already. The green box is like a green light, it's go-mode all the time. Achieve, achieve, achieve.

It's especially important to fill yourself up with positive words in this space, or even to get to this green box, because word selection is vital to what our brain hears, thinks, and processes.

So a man thinketh, so he is. You are what you believe you are. If you think you can, you are already there. You know, the sayings and wisdom we have heard all of our lives actually have validity; challenge your internal dialogue and your thinking.

Effort, energy, and attitude are paramount to what our day will really be like. And here's the beautiful thing about EEA: We are in control of our effort 100%. We control our energy 100%. We control our attitude 100%. Life truly is 10% of what happens and 90% of how we respond to what happens.

For example, someone may say, "Oh, I got fired from my job," and they can paint that as a disaster or a tragedy or very negative news. Or they can say, "You know, I lost my job, and that's not the best thing in the world to happen, but it gives me an opportunity to look for other opportunities, to shift gears and look at changing industries, occupations, or other pursuits. You know what? This could be a golden opportunity for me," versus someone who would postulate that as a negative experience with a grave impact to their life.

In turn, someone can say, "Well, I went through a divorce." You could frame it in the red box, and you might say, "Oh my gosh, it's so hard, so difficult; it's so challenging." It is. As someone who has gone through divorce myself, I understand, it is very challenging on many levels. But you can also learn from the outcome, and that's the golden moment we have in any life moment or difficult event. You have a decision point, a moment, a small sliver of time when you get to decide. How am I going to frame this? Am I going to frame it in the positive light? Am I going to frame it in the negative light? Am I going to take a step back and see it as a separate event, separate from who I am as a person, not something that defines me or my life from one life occurrence? Events do not need to be negatively life-altering. When we alter our thoughts and perceptions, we can harness that energy and then frame our mindset to see the event and respond to it in strength and growth.

The choice is ours, in any circumstance, in every moment in time. There's a point in our lives that we must make a choice to change and say, "I'm not going to live life in a negative way from a negative mindset anymore. I'm not going to live life in self-doubt or with the glass half empty. I'm going to live my life with intention, in a very positive and fruitful way."

I say, "Be on your way with your EEA." It's a little reminder that we have a choice daily to affect our effort, energy, and attitude. We can control these three elements for positive outcomes of life's experiences.

DECISION POINT

When we talk about the psychology of a world champion, it essentially means the way a world champion thinks and the elements that impact that way of thinking, which ultimately impacts peak performance. The way a world champion communicates in their daily practices and protocols, we have learned, really starts with the thoughts. We have explored a scientific chain of the way thoughts lead to behavior and that one's thoughts impact feelings, feelings lead to mood, and mood leads to behavior.

There is one more element that builds that foundation of what we call self-efficacy: It's a belief system, a strong belief system, in oneself and their ability to execute behaviors and perform in particular ways to achieve specific goals. Self-efficacy is developed throughout childhood and adolescence until about 24 to 26 years of age, when the prefrontal cortex is completely developed in executive functioning, like decision-making and planning.

Self-efficacy is built through a psychological ecosystem that I believe has two levels: micro, which is your immediate family, and macro, which is the people with whom you come in contact but maybe not on a daily basis, including teachers, coaches, mentors, cousins, relatives, neighbors, or anyone of influence in your community. They're not your micro ecosystem, the people you see every day like immediate family members, but they make up your macro ecosystem and are the external factor that impacts you in meaningful ways, shaping your thoughts, ideas, behaviors, beliefs, and core values.

As a leader, you have to know all of these elements are at play but that you always have the choice to influence them and choose how they will play out. Leaders are born the moment they choose to become one, to make higher choices, to show up fully in life, to make the touchdowns every time opportunities of life present themselves. You get to be the champion of your life when you choose

46

to be. No other option is as fulfilling, and until you do, you are not living life at 212°.

It's time to get fired up and live life to the fullest, at 212°, every day, because we all know this: Everyone dies, but not everyone lives.

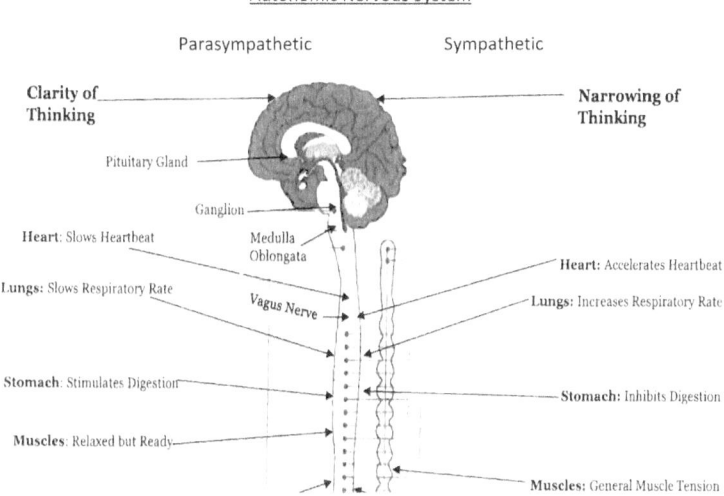

The Autonomic Nervous System is the governing body of the four elements that influence anxiety and depression. Thinking, heart rate, respiration (breathing) and muscle tension are the primary elements that indicate what side of communication and behavior we are deploying. My goal as a Performance Psychologist is to help my clients regulate their anxiety so they can remain on the parasympathetic (predominately) side for optimal performance, both somatically (Body) and cognitively (thinking).

Chapter Four

WHEN FATHERS LOVE

There was an unspeakable bond of admiration and love I had for my dad. He was the steady rock of our family. He set the standard for leadership and certainly impacted my development and self-efficacy, always pushing me to higher standards. He had this desire to drive us harder so that we could go further than he ever had.

He had very high expectations for us. He had a third-grade education, having been forced to quit school in the third grade to work on the family farm. My dad came from a large family, and they had a lot of mouths to feed. The children were expected work, so that's what his dad made him do. In that era, it was the norm, not an exception. Although my dad was extremely bright, he would not be able to flex his intellect until later in his teens. Further, our Spanish heritage stipulated that work was the only way to get ahead. Historically, the Spanish conquistadors (soldiers) were known to be some of the most focused and dedicated fighters of their time.

He grew up in Southern Colorado in what's called the San Louis Valley area, surrounding Alamosa and Manassa, Colorado. In those days it was seen as functional to have every available hand to work the land and to farm and harvest crops. My grandpa needed help, so who better to help him than his son?

Well, the price to pay for that is the trade-off of formal education; this would eventually catch up with my dad. However, my dad was able to compensate for this and outsmart his circumstances; he was very industrious in his thinking. When he turned 16 years old, he started realizing that if he didn't do something and be proactive, he may be stuck in the valley without much opportunity outside of farming. He wanted more for himself.

He envisioned not only his life, but also the family he would have some day. He already knew that he wanted to give them a good life and a beautiful opportunity to become educated, unlike what he was offered. So he fabricated his age to get into the Civilian Conservation Corp. or CCs.

The CCs were guys that were the foundational aspect to the military. They did things like dig the roads that were paved for the military's use. It was a lot of hard labor, digging holes for fence posts and establishing infrastructure – work that was truly back-breaking work. He did that for two years, until he turned 18, and then he entered the service (U.S. Army), and that was probably one of the best experiences of his life. Although he didn't realize it at the time, he understood it later in life.

He traveled all over the world. He was in Germany, France, Spain, and in many different countries for his work in the military. He was honorably discharged about four or five years later. One of the things he learned in the service was mathematics. He learned how to read and write during his time in the military and how to be a functional member of society, making up for all his lack of education.

My dad took his third-grade education and stretched himself to obtain a vast informal education, if you will, from the military. But his formal education was third-grade level. And one of the things I'm most proud of in my journey is that, in one generation, we went from a third-grade education to a Ph.D. level of intellect. It really was one of the greatest days of my life when I could tell my dad that I had been conferred the degree of Doctor of Philosophy in Psychology (Ph.D.) and I was now considered a doctor. He was very proud of that.

He always tuned in to listen to me on the radio and TV, and he would let me know that made him very proud. He would say, "Rick, you're a pretty smart guy you know. I truly enjoy listening to you on the radio." I'm glad I could give him that pleasure, having lost two children in his life; I was glad it helped to ease some of the pain he carried. I looked up to my dad tremendously. We weren't rich by any stretch of the imagination, but we had enough, and we definitely had enough love, and that went around. My mom was an amazing human being, and so was my dad. I truly came from an amazing family, and I am very grateful for my parents.

I must add, I've been around great leaders – some of the biggest names in sports, in terms of coaches and players. I've been around some of the greatest leaders in the academic world, some of the godfathers of psychology who were teaching at Harvard as I studied, and then also in the business world. I've been around some big names with celebrity status, some real titans in that world, and yet, I can honestly say the two greatest human beings I've ever known are my mom and my dad.

They persevered through losing not one, but two children – I had a sister before Danny who was born with polio and passed away at the age of 12, before I was born. Losing two children, one to murder and one to a deadly disease, must have been excruciatingly painful. However, like the thesis of this book, they were able to turn tragedy into beauty. Their energy, passion, and conviction for life clearly rained down on me every day, and I am so thankful that they found the grace of God to carry them through. For them, religion helped them make sense of their losses.

THE MOMENT LEADERS ARE BORN

Despite those great tragedies, they were able to still have a great attitude, raise a family, keep persevering through life, and control their effort, energy, and attitude, and the way they showed up for us was phenomenal. I've always looked up to my dad, and I have tremendous respect for him. He lived to be 99 years old; that is quite a testimony of a life well lived, running the race with endurance. Two months before he passed, I remember saying to him, "If I could be half the man that you are, Dad, then I will have achieved a lot."

He looked at me and said, "You know, Son, look at all you've achieved. You've become a Collegiate All-American, you played in the NFL, you achieved the highest level of education you can achieve. You have done so much with your life."

He was right, but while sitting in front of my Dad in his last moments, those achievements seemed so hollow. And knowing all my Dad had accomplished in his life and the standard he gave for our family, I wanted to offer him so much more.

"Dad, those are achievements," I said, and I felt it in my gut. "That's very different than who I am as a man."

I still strive to be the man that he was and live up to the example he set and the standard he raised for our family. He was just an amazing human being.

One of the greatest experiences that I had as a son of my dad was sharing in his love for farm life. My dad grew up on a farm, so it was something for him that seemed like home, as it was a part of him. Although we lived in the city, in Denver he still yearned for a farm, to work the land, to introduce us to that way of life.

So, when I was eight, he purchased five acres of land north of Denver, about 20 to 30 miles outside of the city, in the small town of Brighton, Colorado, in Weld County. We bought some horses, cows, and pigs, we had chickens and rabbits, and it was just like the good old days for my dad. It was like the farm of his childhood. He could relax there and enjoy his family by his side.

On the weekends we'd go to the farm, and during the week we'd live the city life in Denver. We had neighbors next to the farm that would help us out and give water to the horses and the livestock while we were away, and then on the weekends we'd go out there and get our hands dirty and care for the animals. And it wasn't an option for me to go to the farm. It was mandatory. My dad was firm about having the entire family participate.

"No, you're going and you're going to help me. We're going to build some sheds. We're going to build some barns, and it's what we're going to do." He was always so gung-ho, and he made it very clear that my participation was not optional.

So, I learned early on how to use a hammer and nails, how to work with power tools, and most importantly, I learned accountability. I learned that structure, responsibility, and discipline are important, and I learned that my dad had high expectations for me. He was growing me as a leader without me even realizing it.

I'll give you one example. He used to fill up a seven-gallon bucket of water. A gallon of water weighs about eight pounds, and if you multiply that times seven, that's about a 55-to-60-pound bucket of water. When I first started going out to the farm with my dad, I was about eight-and-a-half years old. I honestly think my dad purchased this property as a way to get his mind away from the pain and the agony that he endured from losing a second child, especially to murder.

So, he would fill up this bucket and then purposely call me over and point to it, saying, "Okay, bring it to where I am." Then he'd walk a hundred meters away. There was no physical way that I could carry that 60-pound bucket of water like someone grown typically would with one arm and one hand. I had to grab it with two hands, two arms in the middle of the thin, metal handle, and with my legs straddling to the outside of the heavy, metal bucket. I had to take the bucket, step by step, one baby shuffle step at a time. I could do that for two or three steps, and then I would have to put it down and rest to look at my hand, where there was a big, red mark from the metal handle. But I would keep at it, two or three steps at a time, holding my breath, biting my bottom lip, determined to show my dad that I could, and then put it down.

He knew what he was doing. He knew that at first I would not be able to carry that big bucket full of water, but he wanted to stretch me. He wanted to push me. And through that challenge, I learned to dig deeper and push myself and eventually get that – still mostly full – bucket of water to him to pour in the animal's troughs. He was patient; he never intervened to help me carry it or give me a way out. He set the expectation and was patient until I fulfilled the challenge. My overall body strength became advanced for my age, no doubt due to my work on the farm.

It's unfortunate now because he's gone, but he did have so many stories, and I would like to have him retell them to me and to continue to share those memories with him. I recall when he would tell us about his childhood memories of feeding the livestock in spite of the brutal winter temperatures. Their family farm was in the valley, and it would sometimes get to be 20 degrees below zero; there were times he couldn't even feel his feet or his fingers. The animals had to be cared for in spite of the conditions. He certainly did build character – there were no excuses. It's amazing he never got frostbite.

As a result, my dad had high expectations for me. And that "water walk" – that's what I call it – was amazing training for me. Actually, looking back on it now, it trained me not only emotionally and psychologically, but it trained me physically. And I don't think it's any mystery that several years later in high school, I set the all-time record for the bench press, which still stands to this day, some 40 years later. I guess "water walks" are excellent for building muscles and body strength.

Going to the farm added layers of richness to my life; some effects I was not aware of at the time. It built accountability and offered structure in my life. But the other thing it did was build a bond between my dad and me. He didn't talk about my brother's death very much. He didn't talk about the loss of Barbara, my sister. But that time we spent together, driving in his truck on the way out there and back to the city again, spending the day together, sharing lunch together, simple little things, like when we'd see a garden snake or a bull snake and he'd show me how to kill it, those were the moments that made my childhood special and our time together pretty amazing. He would show me to just take a shovel and sever its head. He showed me how to manage the animals and even butcher the animals to use the meat. It's not that we needed it for survival. We went to grocery stores for our food. But it was a great way to get a whole winter's worth of pork or beef and store up food.

I watched the process as a company would come butcher the animals, process their meat, cure it, and package it for us. He also taught me how to do that with rabbits with my bare hands. It's not for the faint of heart but a normal way of life on a farm, and for us. This was something I also learned on the Navajo reservation, or more affectionately known as the "Rez." My cousin, Ben, lived on the Rez in Shiprock, New Mexico and showed me and my other cousins how to butcher rabbits with our bare hands. My dad also taught me this practice on our farm, and it no doubt taught me some cultural practices congruent with our Navajo heritage. They literally showed me how to break their necks with one strike and then skin the rabbits and prepare them for cooking. Being that I was only about nine the first time I attempted to butcher a rabbit, I was afraid to "hurt" the animal. But in no time my native side took over, and I understood that I had a right-of-passage to experience, and that was to supply food for my family. To this day, I have a real sense of taking care of those I love; I firmly believe it comes from my dad's and cousins' teachings on the farm and the 'Rez' (reservation).

Those practices taught me a lot – about managing a farm, handling livestock, the nitty gritty of what goes into animals as sustenance and the processing of food. I look back now and recall that I didn't want to kill a rabbit. I didn't want to break its neck with my bare hands. But it was something he required me to do because it was necessary for taking care of the farm, for survival, and that's what his father taught him on the farm when he was younger. It was kind of heartbreaking for me because I looked at rabbits as pets more than food, but it was part of farm life. It also taught me a level of respect for animals. There is a pecking order in the food chain. It was part of my culture and my heritage, as well. It all took me back to my roots in the native world of how Mother Earth is used to supply food and nutrition for everybody in our clan. Eventually, I came to understand it. It kept me accountable, and it helped me to grow into a man. I respect my dad for teaching me these things. These are just a few of the memories I have of my Dad teaching me skills and exposing me to life that helped me grow as a man and as a leader.

I've been called upon many times to be a leader. I attribute some of this to my development through life experiences so early in life. Early on in my career, from football, where I was tasked to be a captain and a leader to the team, and so on, like compensating for Danny's death and choosing to be strong for my mom at such a young age.

I just always took that responsibility and ran with it. It never was a burden to me. It was never like, "I don't want to speak in front of the team." It was an opportunity for me to do so, and I think it goes back to those experiences on the farm with my dad and all of his expectations of me, high expectations of me to do simple, everyday tasks without complaining and without question.

Needless to say, when my dad passed away in the fall 2019, at 99 years old, it was still, believe it or not, unexpected. It was very, very tough to accept and process, and it still is to this day. He was a titan of a man and a role model to me. At 99 years old, he was still perfectly healthy. He'd had a few hiccups along the road, like in his early to mid- nineties when he'd fallen down and broken a hip, but for the most part, he was very healthy; he was still very much a strong work horse and taking care of himself.

On the day that he died, he made his bed, prepared his breakfast, sat down to eat, and the best estimate we have is that he passed away sitting up at the table, probably between 8:00 and 10:00 a.m. It's when my sister found him, still sitting at the table, about 5:00 p.m. that same day, that we had to acknowledge his time with us was over. We accepted that he had gone to see his wife, my mom, Annie.

When titans die, it's a huge deal. My dad was a titan. He was a man among men, not in size, but in what mattered most. My dad was a relatively small guy in size, but in heart and spirit, in love and trust, all these key elements of great character and self-efficacy, he was a titan. A titan of a man.

He dedicated himself to his family every day. He did everything he could every day to build his family and to provide for us and to connect with each one of us. And even after losing two children, Barbara and Danny, he had a great attitude, he had great energy, and a great passion to continue to lead his family. For me, a titan died on September 24th, 2019. That day will never change in my mind. I'll never forget when I answered a phone call from my sister, and I knew from her tone of voice that it was a different kind of phone call. You know, our dad was so resilient that I thought he was going to live to be 102 or 103, easy. So when I got that phone call and I heard a different inflection in her voice, I immediately thought it was maybe one of her children, maybe one of them had been in an accident or something.

When she asked, "Rick, where are you?" I knew something was different.

"I'm driving," I said, my eyes darting in the rear-view mirror to check my kids' faces.

"Okay," she said, pausing. Not being able to contain herself, she continued, "Rick, Dad passed away today."

I'll never forget hearing her voice crack or receiving that call, because it wasn't just me in the car hearing this news for the first time. I was in my car and I had just picked up my 16-year-old son (Kaleb) from football practice, and my 13-year-old (Keegan) son was in the car too. Immediately I heard both the boys sniffling in the back seat and whimpering from Keegan because the speaker was on Bluetooth and they heard what she had said at the same moment I heard it.

I knew eventually this day was coming. I just didn't know it would be so soon. You see, we were already beginning to plan his 100th birthday party. His 99th birthday was such an amazing get-together, and we were planning to top it off with a 100th birthday celebration to remember. But he had other plans. He decided to go see his beautiful bride, Annie; it was time.

I drove immediately to his house. My sister was there with her husband, Gary, and their family, and the coroner was there. He described, with his best assumption, "Your father died sitting up in the chair."

Even on the day he passed he was still making himself breakfast, taking care of himself, going through the discipline of daily life and his routine.

And then, the next thing the coroner said was a little harder to process, "But for him to be taken away to the mortuary, we need to straighten him out." And so, they straightened him out and laid him down on the floor, right there in front of us. He was straight and stoic, heroic, even in death.

So, my sister, who is an oncology nurse, and myself, both helpers of people, were escorted in to address my dad's body. Nothing prepares you for this. It was nothing less than shocking to see this titan of a man lying on the kitchen floor with no life running through his body. I didn't even know how to process that. I didn't even know how to conceptualize that. It was something very different than I'd ever seen in my whole life. My sister immediately began to cry, and then I did too. It was one of the most gripping moments in my life, and I'll always remember it.

What really became salient for me was when we decided to let the children come in. My children, Kaleb and Keegan, were there with me. Keegan, my 13-year-old, walked in the room, took one look at my dad, and fell to his knees and started crying very hard, just sobbing.

"I can't believe it," he said. "I can't believe he's gone." He impulsively touched him, as if to prove it to himself. He touched his hand. And at that moment I realized I was looking at three generations of Perea men communicating verbally and nonverbally through pure, raw emotion. At that moment I realized the titan of a man – my dad, my son's grandpa – had just died. I will forever be touched by that moment and the whole experience of that day.

THE MOMENT LEADERS ARE BORN

Experiencing that with my sons also did something to me. Through that experience, we all matured a little and stepped into a new season of life. I knew then, as I always had but on an even deeper level right then in that moment, that I wanted to be half the father to my sons that my dad was to me. That day just further cemented that to me in my whole being – that being a father, a great father, who always shows up for my sons, is now my driving force and the most important thing in the world to me. That's the kind of legacy my dad left, and that's the kind of father and leader he groomed me to be, and I am determined to leave that same legacy for my sons. I love you Dad…

Chapter Five

CHAMPION OF RELATIONSHIPS

Throughout our lives, we go through many different relationships, beginning with birth, when our parents take care of us. Growing up with peers, friendships, interpersonal relationships, romantic relationships – the connections are endless. The relationships that we go through in life have an impact on our perception, including attitudes, beliefs, and cultural values.

We only get one chance to make it right (so it seems), to show up as our best self, and to fully enjoy relational benefits. So many of us make a go of it, and for whatever reason – poor timing, circumstances, wrong mate, world issues – we just don't quite get it right; we are not on the same linear path, and at the crossroads of life, there is a complete heart disconnection that has the potential to derail our identities, disrupt our lives, and potentially damage even our futures.

And, to further complicate the path of two individuals whose lives have dramatically shifted from the future they envisioned, many in the world suddenly have an opinion or an emotion to share.

Oftentimes in our society, when you tell people you are divorced or going through a divorce, they take that with a negative connotation. The word *divorce*, the denotation, is, "to divide, separate, dissociate." I challenge you to look at divorce in another way: from a perspective I have personally experienced. Before we delve into the contextualism of divorce, I want to clearly state that while I feel divorce can be a catalyst for development and growth, I encourage couples to seek coaching and/or counseling to make every effort to heal the wounds that can impale a union intrinsically.

When cells divide, that's actually considered growth, not a negative pattern. I want you to understand that, oftentimes when people divorce, that can be a signal and a reflection of growth and development as well. While many people will gloat and talk about their 30-year, 40-year marriage as a badge of honor, oftentimes those marriages are spent in dysfunction; physical, mental, emotional abuse; and angles of emotional leveraging that really don't grow the partner or the partnership.

While it's not a mainstream thought, it's what I want to explore – not so much the divide of divorce as a format for growth, but how relationships grow us and shape us and make a lasting impact. What I challenge you to really look at in yourself is your own relationships and the various dynamics. All relationships have an impact on us to some degree.

For example, we can look at friendships and interpersonal relationships on an even more personal emotional level, on a romantic level, such as with a boyfriend, girlfriend, husband, or wife. As you evaluate each one, does that relationship grow you? Relationships shape us, challenge us, impact us, stretch us, test us, and eventually help us to change and grow into a better version of ourselves.

After a period of my life, I was reflecting on working with some of my clients, and they would come in and refer to their families as broken, fractured, dysfunctional, or divorced, and state that in some way their families weren't as solid or as functional as one that had never been fractured, divorced, or divided. In other words, they made the oversimplification that just because their family went through a divorce, they were somehow at a sociological disadvantage. Many families that have decided to part ways (between partners), are more intrinsically healthy than ones that have "endured" the test of time.

I became leery of hearing the oversimplification regarding relationships because, through my practice, I have heard many first-hand accounts, and they tend to be oversimplified which limits our perceptual base. I know people that have been through one divorce, two divorces, even three divorces that will look back on their lives and say that those experiences grew them, tested them, challenged them, and developed them as people and helped them evolve into the people they are today. The relationships they had experienced also had an impact on their children. Often, growth occurred on many levels.

Today the research is very clear: Divorce does not hurt children. It does not necessarily impact children in a negative way. I think it's imperative that we understand that it's not divorce in and of itself that can be a challenge or harmful to the children. It's the way parents handle the divorce. I personally would like to talk about how divorce has impacted my life.

I look at myself and I think it would be healthy for all of us to look at ourselves and the relationships we commit to from a long-term perspective, a lifespan. You go through different stages in life, and it's somewhat unrealistic to think that you will meet the one partner that fits you for the span of your entire life. Perhaps you make a decision in your 20s and 30s, and you assess where you are emotionally, psychologically, developmentally, educationally, and so on, and think that that person is going to be a fit for you going forward throughout your lifespan.

THE MOMENT LEADERS ARE BORN

The changes experienced by both individuals are not accounted for in this time of early relationships. You make an effort to continually learn and grow and develop, then there is change to the individual, and in turn, to the couple. There is no doubt about it. There are a multitude of different emotional, psychological, and even physical changes that show up and impact a relationship. The question becomes how someone adapts to that. How do you adjust to that within a relationship? How do you adapt to having children when your partner decides to employ a parenting style that contradicts yours? Many parents (as was the case in my marriage) assert that they will be structured and disciplined and then when children are born and raised do not adhere to that style and become more laissez-faire in their parenting style. How do you account for this change? You don't; you either adapt to it or make the realization that the parenting styles conflict.

Oftentimes in a relationship in which agreements are made, whether it be a formal agreement, like marriage, or an informal agreement, like common law marriage or as a committed partner, we later find that the two parties are growing in different directions, maybe at different rates and on different levels. And at one point or another, we have to make a decision whether it is a healthy relationship as we see it going forward for ourselves and our future. In my marriage I often felt emotionally captive, like I was not able to express my emotions freely the way I wanted to with humor, spontaneity and emotional intimacy.

I liken the interaction of human communication to a swimming pool. There's the ten-foot pool that you dive into, and there's a drain down at the bottom, and that's the deep end. And you have the eight-foot, six-foot, and three-foot variations in depth, as well. There are a lot of people who exist in the three-foot depth in the pool, and some people even cling to the side and kind of slide their hands along the side because they're very careful of how they navigate in the pool, full of fear and anxiety, not willing to let go and swim freely. Now, looking at my life, having been on this earth a half century, I choose to dive into the deep end of the pool, and I like to hover down around the drain and explore as well.

We all have different levels of comfort and areas of growth, different willingness to risk things for growth and to live life more freely. When we talk about relationships, I want to be very clear that oftentimes relationships and the divide of a relationship is a clear reflection on development and growth of one or both individuals and the varying levels of risk and freedom one individual is willing to take, not a reflection of failure on the part of either party. In our society we tend to oversimplify that.

Leaders and champions often face setbacks; they experience the trials and tribulations just like everyone else does. And oftentimes these trials and tribulations are experienced in quiet and solitude in the dark because many leaders and champions think that they socially cannot show that they are vulnerable in everyday life. But in fact, when you lead, you put yourself in a more vulnerable state. When you become a champion, you become more visible, usually more vocal and more verbal. In these leadership positions, it's easy to be exposed to high-risk communication and high-risk behavior. So I think it's important to understand how germane it is to acknowledge that leaders and champions do face setbacks in their lives – interpersonal and professional challenges, in their own relationships, and so on – and that we must process and reflect on every aspect of the factors involved and really turn the experience into beauty. That is the true center of leadership – being honest in our relationships, to ourselves, and truly stepping back to evaluate what's going on, owning it and acknowledge it and seeing it for what it is rather than simply dismissing it, acting tough, brushing it under the rug, ignoring it, or blaming the other person. Instead, leaders lead with authenticity, communication, truth, and understanding for all parties involved. Acknowledge it for what it is and see the growth in that.

How do you become a champion in the face of adversity, trauma, and even tragedy? My supposition is that it actually takes a trial, a tribulation, or a tragedy to bring out the best in a person and reveal their true self.

You know the sayings out there – "You don't know the real person until he/she has been tested by the fire, and that reveals the true version of himself/herself," or "There is not a testimony without a test." Oftentimes the hardest trials are the experiences that make us look deep within and really make us leave our comfort zone to take a truer look at ourselves and the truth that has just revealed. Exercising your comfort zone is a technique that we teach in my practice, and we express, number one, that you have to be willing to experience discomfort. If you're not willing to experience discomfort emotionally and psychologically, you will rarely make the change that is necessary to achieve excellence and greatness. We also recommend that you leave your comfort zone five times a day – try it on, feel it out, stretch yourself.

Now, that doesn't mean that you have to leave your comfort zone in dramatic ways five times a day – some small, some bigger. Something simple like trying a new food is leaving your comfort zone. Another way of leaving your comfort zone is wearing a color that you never have before. A third way to leave your comfort zone would be to approach somebody that you would have hesitated to approach in the past, whether it be an authority figure, somebody like a teacher or professor, or even somebody you may have an interest in that you hesitated to approach before because you thought they may reject you in some way.

It's sometimes said that we ended up with our second- or third-teamer as our intimate partner. What that means is that we'll rarely go after our first-teamer. Our first-teamer is the person that we look at and say, "Wow, that's somebody that I would really like to meet." Now, it's a bit oversimplified to say we're just attracted by a person's looks, so we will be attracted to them, but I think it's fair to say that oftentimes we'll approach somebody that we perceive to be "on our level" in terms of looks, so I think it's important to understand that leaving your comfort zone five times a day means you begin to be comfortable being uncomfortable. When you're comfortable being uncomfortable, you have made it to a new place, a place of growth, and that's a pretty great place to be. That essentially means that you're very rarely uncomfortable. Now you are free to show up as yourself, without inhibition or restriction.

There's beauty in the struggle, and it is helpful to also see things from other people's viewpoints. When you're very ethnocentric and egocentric, you tend to look at things from your viewpoint and your viewpoint only. Our experiences color our world, our experiences are comfortable for us, they're safe for us. But we can suspend those thoughts, feelings, and perceptions, that ethnocentricity, and practice a technique called *epoché*, a Greek word for suspension of judgment, and look at other people's viewpoints, how they see things.

Recently I went to dinner with a friend of mine on Valentine's Day, and it really wasn't because of the significance of the day that we went out to dinner; it just happened to be a time when we both were free, which just so happened to be Valentine's Day. I was sharing this idea with another friend of mine, but from the outside looking in, she thought it was going to look like I went for a romantic dinner on Valentine's Day. When I stopped and thought about it, it made sense. But from my viewpoint, I missed that because that was not my intent. "No, it's just another day. I'm just taking time out to have dinner with a friend and it just happens to be a day that we're both free; there is no correlation to the day marked *Valentine's*." Oftentimes in life we have to stop and slow down and practice *epoché* so that we can see things from other viewpoints, not just our own.

The fourth thing I want us to understand is that growth occurs when we feel discomfort. You know, on a physiological level, when cells divide, we grow. And growth occurs when we feel discomfort both emotionally and psychologically.

The other day I was at the dermatologist with my son, and she asked to see his back. He had a simple case of acne, and she wanted to see if he had acne on his back. When she pulled up his shirt, it looked like there were a multitude of scratches across his back. I said to my son, "How come your back is all scratched up?"

The dermatologist looked at me, and she said, "Those are stretch marks. He's in a growth spurt right now. He's growing." And it's just like that when we experience growth. It feels uncomfortable when we're in a growth spurt. The knees hurt, the back hurts, the body is changing, inside we might feel angst, a pull and tug of the shift that is happening. It's the same thing psychologically and emotionally. When we're growing, it's discomfort.

We have to leave our comfort zone to get to that place we want to be. If we always stay in our comfort zone, we'll never grow. We'll never grow exponentially like we want to so we can experience success and be great leaders of our life.. If you think of the cocoon and the caterpillar and the butterfly, the cocoon is a really safe place to be, and I get it, but what's the view like inside the cocoon? Now, the butterfly, once it breaks outside of the cocoon, has a beautiful view. But it's a little dangerous out there in the world, too. There's prey, and you have to expose yourself to some dangers out there. But what would you rather do: live in the cocoon, nice and safe with a very limited viewpoint, or would you live the life of a butterfly, vast and free and open, yet exposed to some new environmental factors, maybe even danger?

In terms of facing the setback and turning it into beauty, first there's a prerequisite of discomfort; to perform at your highest levels, you must feel discomfort. That is the setback. The challenges in life that can appear to be setbacks or the slow steps to victory and the growth we seek, are actually the set-up for the transition of change. You know, through this book we talk about people who have been through tragedy, trauma – like myself with the murder of my brother or like some of my dear friends, who I have invited to participate in this story with me, who have experienced the murder of a sister, or like a high-powered attorney who had a double mastectomy surgery in what seems like far too devastating a setback, or a leader in talk radio for decades who lost his son to suicide but has embraced the experience for growth and to bring beauty to others from his story – but they each evolved into beautiful people, transformed into butterflies, so to speak, who now experience a level of beauty, freedom and growth that was previously unavailable to their perceptual values.

And this is why we postulate in our practice that a prerequisite of performance is discomfort. I can personally tell you that the biggest growth period I had in my life was when my brother Danny was murdered. And then, in another way, when during my Ph.D. program I was really pressed to the limit in so many ways – time-wise, organization-wise – stretching my capacity to perform, testing my drive, motivation, and understanding of the science to which I was being exposed. There were times when, during the dissertation phase of my program, my committee challenged me to make my dissertation more scientific. I was examining the essence of the human experience of different levels of culture and culture's effect on performance. I had to go through a certain level of discomfort to be able to achieve that level of performance and expectation. I was bringing everything I had to the table, and they continued to ask for more. It stretched me to a very high level of performance and forced me to grow to meet these expectations.

Above all of this performance and growth and stretching is the defining factor of how we think that will ultimately mold us into the leaders and champions we are striving to be. If we approach every morning with a willingness to search for discomfort, search for leaving our comfort zone to improve and not run from it, then that'll be a norm for us, the way we think. Leaders choose the "road less traveled" for a reason. If it was the easy way, everyone would do it. If we wake up every morning and our number one goal is to be safe and stay inside our cocoon, then we're really never going to reach our true potential in life. How many times has it happened to you that you were going to go talk to a particular person or a particular group and then when you finally did get the courage to do it, you stopped and said, "Wow, I should have approached that person long before because they're actually very friendly, and it was much easier than I expected."

So, oftentimes we'll make assessments and judgments based on how people look, how they act, their skin color, their cultural practices and norms, as opposed to actually knowing the person and getting to know who they are and their approachability, for example. So how we think will determine our level of comfort and discomfort, what that means to us, and then ultimately being able to be comfortable being uncomfortable.

DECISION POINT

As leaders, we have to figure out how to maneuver the play when the playbook changes. Life is full of curveballs, but winning or growing in the process should always be our main objective. Basically, to play to win means doing a couple of things that are really going to help us stay on a consistent emotional and psychological plane, and that is using mindfulness and emotional intelligence as we approach our activities. When the playbook changes and the path we are on takes a sharp turn or we get off course due to unexpected life events, oftentimes our thoughts can really play games with us. The first thing I want people to understand is that thoughts are not facts. Thoughts are *not* facts. The average human being has 45,000 thoughts a day and up to 75% of those thoughts are negative. That leaves us 33,000 thoughts a day that are not necessarily great thoughts. Those are random thoughts. And if we choose purposeful thoughts instead, we get to control those negative thoughts that have the potential to derail us and flip them to positive thoughts. I challenge you to shape your thoughts because if you do not, your thoughts will shape you.

The first aspect is recognizing that thoughts are not facts. We have very many random thoughts that are often dark, deficit-based – thoughts of self-doubt and negativity. They're not facts. We need to test them and quickly dismiss them, reframe them to work to our advantage. Our mindset must be sharp and positive.

Mindfulness also predicates that we have moment-by-moment awareness instead of doubt, fear or anxiety, worrying about tomorrow. Don't let yesterday or tomorrow rob you of today. Just live fully in the moment, moment by moment, and take a "be where your feet are" approach.

The next aspect of the mindset of a champion is accepting uncomfortable thoughts. Oftentimes we have uncomfortable thoughts that seep into our brain, and they can be things that are really dark or disturbing or full of self-doubt or fear-based. When we fight those thoughts, that equates to frustration and anger, and the internal struggle becomes evident. Take every thought captive, one by one, and defeat them or turn them around to a positive before you accept them.

Hurt and fear are primary emotions; anger and frustration are secondary emotions. When we accept the uncomfortable thought, we're in that parasympathetic side of the autonomic nervous system, the calm side, which really helps us achieve at high levels. Accepting uncomfortable thoughts is really one of our objectives in mindfulness. This type of thinking will help us to grow and see the negative thoughts for the imposters that they are.

Pay close attention to your senses, your sensory processing. We have five senses and essentially six with intuition. The more senses that we have stimulated, the more mindful and the more present we are. If you've ever been hiking or swimming in the ocean or walking on the beach, you may have felt a more heightened self-awareness because more of our senses are engaged. The smell of the ocean or the fresh mountain air, the touch of nature or the grains of sand, the sound of the ocean waves or the birds in the rustling trees, and obviously the visual stimulation from the brilliance of our surroundings – the more senses that we can stimulate, the more mindful and the more present we will be in our moments, the more aware of our feelings and breathing and thinking and so on.

So, when the playbook changes and life throws you a curveball, go back to those moments in your mind where you were fully present. Take a few slow, deep, calming breaths. Make yourself fully aware and centered in the moment. Be very present in your thoughts, very mindful, recognize where the negative thoughts come from, and then take authority to shape them so they don't shape you or your circumstances.

The next aspect is emotional intelligence. Emotional intelligence (EI) is an important factor because it means that we need to be aware of how emotions play a role in performance and impact us in every aspect of communication and behavior. When we're on that sympathetic side of the autonomic nervous system, we have an increased heart rate, increased breathing, respiration, muscle tension, and narrowing of thinking; we do not think as clear.

For example, when we say things that are hurtful to people, we're in the sympathetic side of the autonomic system. What we mostly realize to be EI is the ability to self-regulate, to slow down and self-adjust so we can really be in a place of performance that helps us achieve at peak levels. In fact, the inability to manage or regulate emotions is at the root of most performance failure.

I once was working with a major league baseball pitcher and his coaches were complaining that he kept dropping his elbow on delivery. They treated that as merely a mechanical issue, but I explained to them that it wasn't just a mechanical issue; it was actually an emotional, psychological issue. I explained to them that, when he perceived the batter was a very good hitter, he would say things to himself like, "Oh no, it's so-and-so. It's Nolan Arenado, it's Carlos González," and that would immediately trigger the pituitary gland, releasing adrenaline, which would activate the sympathetic side of the autonomic nervous system, making him feel muscle tension in his arm. When he felt muscle tension, he would subconsciously pull his elbow closer into his body to get more power.

So, it's really important to understand that we can trace most performance failure back to the sympathetic side of the autonomic nervous system – muscle tension, narrowing of thinking, saying things we don't really mean. Then when we calm down, we're on the parasympathetic side, and we say what we really mean. It's very important to understand that.

The difference between people having success in their lives and not is oftentimes emotional intelligence. It's really sad to think that many of our violent offenders in prison today are there because they were emotionally unintelligent. When I was coming up during my educational experiences, I once did an internship in a couple of medium-security prisons in southern Colorado. I remember really enjoying working with those prisoners and walking out of there thinking to myself, "Man, these are good people; they just made bad decisions." Oftentimes I heard those inmates say, "If I had not been so upset, I wouldn't have pulled that trigger, I wouldn't have stabbed that person, I wouldn't have punched that person," or whatever it may have been. Emotional intelligence is a big factor when it comes to adjusting to when the playbook changes. Great leaders and great performers use mindfulness, emotional intelligence, and leaving their comfort zone to reach high levels of performance.

The final aspect to being a champion of a relationship is to lead as a father. We've talked earlier about relationships. I've been a father for some 32 years now. And it's really interesting because I view it as my most important role, even more important than a partnership with my romantic partner because, as a father, I have responsibility, I have accountability, and I am their primary role model.

I made a big decision in my career recently. I've been very fortunate to work in the National Football League, Major League Baseball, and the National Basketball Association. But as my sons moved into middle adolescence, I recognize the need for me to be a great father, a father at home, one that could really be active in their lives and their experiences. For me, it was a choice to lead as a father.

DECISION POINT

Great leaders are not just leaders in the board room, they're not just great leaders in their organizations or teams, but rather they're great leaders as partners and as fathers. As fathers, we have to make a concerted effort to be there for our sons and our daughters and to make great decisions that support them.

My relationship now with my sons is priceless. They're 17, 14, and 12 and just a joy to be around. Don't get me wrong, there's days that I want to ship them out and send them off to military camp, but for the most part, the vast majority of the time, they're just beautiful human beings that I love being around and shaping every day. We often think we're teaching them about life, but they're actually teaching us about life and ourselves. I've learned more about myself from my children than any textbooks I've ever read.

Being a great father and a leader as a father is so important. I've had some great role models. My father was an amazing human being, an amazing father, a great role model, he always did the right thing, and he always did the right thing for his family.

Coach Larry Tarver, my coach in high school, was a tremendous role model and leader. In high school, he and his wife and his two kids were in a horrific accident that changed his wife's life forever. She had brain injuries and never recovered fully. She had to learn again to walk and talk, and she never looked the same again. But he always stood by his family. Even to this day, we're still close. He has stood by his wife and his family through all those trials and tribulations. A great example of a leader as a father.

Coach Jacob's my defensive coordinator from college, a tremendous leader. He taught me more about leadership than any one human being I can name. But he was also a leader as a father, and to this day he is learning things about himself as a grandfather. In my conversations with him, he shares with me experiences of mindfulness and emotional intelligence, and he's really having to transcend himself to be a great grandfather. But to think about what a great leader he's been as a football coach and as a mentor to us as players, and now to learn so much about himself in his 70s as a grandfather, is really beautiful to hear.

If you're going to be a champion of your relationships, you must understand it's a choice. You have to choose to lead as a father, choose to lead as a grandfather and to make the right decisions for your kids. You don't have to be perfect – no one's perfect as a father – but you have to be excellent, and that means making great choices to support them. Let them see you make mistakes. Don't ever think that you have to be perfect. We make mistakes in life. That's okay. One of the best lessons they can learn is, "You know what? I don't have to be perfect, because Dad's not perfect." Choose to lead as a father. Fatherhood is one of the most beautiful places to be, and my sons right now are my pride and joy. We laugh, we cry, we fight, we wrestle, but man, they are my dawgs. They teach me new things about myself every day – my strongpoints and my blind spots. For that, I am forever indebted to them.

Chapter Six

SHEDDING LIGHT ON A DARK SUBJECT

Shedding light on a dark subject is sensitive, challenging, and heart rendering, but I must address it. I would say 50% to 60% of my clients that come into my practice have experience with some type of anxiety or depression. There is a sharp rise in teen and young adult suicide, and the signs of depression and anxiety in adolescents from 10 to 24 is evident and deeply troubling.

I think that depression and anxiety in teens is becoming an epidemic in the United States. Statistics indicate that about 40% of teens and young adolescents experience depression. Some sites indicate one in every three teens will battle with debilitating anxiety by the time they are 18. And the Wall Street Journal reported a 56% rise in teen and young adolescent suicides between the years of 2007 and 2017. We cannot let this go unaddressed or sweep it under the rug. We must connect with people at a core level and understand where they are, how they are doing and how we can help. I have experienced these topics in my practice and through personal relationships. I wanted to share because, as we talk about relationships, we have to be willing to take a deeper dive in getting to know people, who they are, and where they are, especially when it comes to teens and adolescents who may not express themselves or their emotions clearly or often enough. These feelings can be scary and overwhelming, but again, we must stretch ourselves and be willing to get uncomfortable, and "go there" anyway.

I see an increasing number of youths and young adolescents suffering with some type of anxiety or depression that is being communicated in a very underlying way as performance issues in sports. When we look at a sport performer, we look at their competency in terms of basketball, soccer, football, you name the sport of choice. But oftentimes it's not really the performance within their particular sport that is the issue; it is the underlying anxiety and depression that is impacting their performance.

This subject is of significant importance because it has really taken ahold of our culture in our society in the United States in 2020. I want to chronicle an example of how it has depicted itself here in Denver, Colorado.

There's a high school here that year in and year out has some of the highest test scores in the state; let's call it Alpha high school. This high school is considered one of the best-performing schools in the state, and hence has been deemed a great school by parents, community leaders and received high recognition in the state. The connotative attachment to it is that it's a great school, filled with great teachers, great kids, and it's a high performing school, over all very desirable. While Alpha high school has year after year shown the highest test scores in the state, over the last several years it's also had some of the highest suicide rates.

Conversely, we look at another school across town; we will call it Beta High School, in northeast Denver. Beta consistently has some of the lowest test scores in the state, yet there are consistently zero suicides at this school. Yet, you can walk the halls of Beta and see a fist fight in the halls almost every day – tough kids, tough environment, an expression of negative emotions, yet no suicides from this school.

When you look at these two schools in contrast, Alpha, is deemed as a great school, but the underlying issue of that school is the amount of suicides – and not a lot of people talk about it. Compare that to Beta, which has some of the lowest test scores, a lot of fights on a daily basis, yet no suicides. At Alpha, I would suspect that the kids there tend to internalize their anxiety and depression. At Beta, I presume that kids tend to externalize their anxiety and depression. This manifestation of emotions tends to show up as physical aggression against one another.

In spite of the absence of suicides, Beta is deemed as a "bad school" because people say, "But, oh my gosh, there are fights there every day." It would behoove us to take a step back, check our measuring sticks of success, and then to press in to see what underlying factors of teen and adolescent depression, anxiety, and suicide are truly at play.

The dark secret is that, like many schools across our nation, there are as many issues at Alpha as there are at Beta, but they show themselves differently. One's internal, and the other is external. The expectation of performance, the lack of support emotionally and psychologically, among other factors, truly impacts our youth and lends the opportunity for expansive negative effects. We must be watching, listening, and communicating at all times in order to identify what is truly percolating under the surface and behind the silence.

One of the things that my dear friend Sandy Clough will share in this chapter is his experience with his own son's suicide at the age of 27 and how he was depressed and had experienced anxiety during his adolescent years. We come to understand what that experience looks like and its lifelong impact. It lends insight into a dark topic.

THE MOMENT LEADERS ARE BORN

The hard truth is that there's an escalating suicide rate among our young people in America. This is due to a number of factors and variables; some you may not have been aware.

We're putting more pressure on our youth for performance in sports, academics, even socially. If you look at youth in the sports world today, there are more and more youth that are playing club sports, seeking higher levels of training, and the expectation is to perform at high levels because there's such competition for college scholarships; academic and athletic. The pressures are real; often, their futures are bright, but at what cost?

When I get performers in my practice, they often talk about wanting their kids to play at peak levels or their true potential, but what they don't talk about is the pressure that they're putting on their kids; sometimes unconsciously. Oftentimes when families get started in our performance programs, they're willing to look at that themselves and truly reflect at the pressure they're putting on their kids. I've had parents sit in front of me, women and men, and come to tears because they didn't realize the external pressure that that they were putting on their children and the effect it was having on their child's mental, emotional and even physical health.

We have a great opportunity as a society to realize how we're impacting the interpretation of what kids are expected to do and how that pressure can be adding to the anxiety and depression that kids are feeling. We've got to get better in the mental health community at understanding how anxiety manifests itself in communication and behavior; for example, who is seeking occupations and careers in mental health? We require competency and acumen in the name of formal education and training for mental health professions such as social workers, psychotherapists and psychologists, yet we have no requirements for passion, compassion and engaging personalities that would be extremely effective at reaching our adolescents, especially troubled ones. Regularly, I am able to connect with hard to reach youth by yes, deploying cognitive behavioral techniques and other widely accepted practices and norms in the mental health field, but I have found one of the most effective "tools" at reaching adolescents in our society is to *connect* with them. Music, poems, clothes/fashion, jewelry and other sociologically driven topics tend to reach them on their level. That's the key; reach them on their level not ours. When we do little to change our pedagogical delivery system to fit their needs there is usually a disconnect.

Recently, I had a 14 year-old female's mom contact our practice wanting to her daughter to meet me. She had watched me on TV recently on a show called Broncos Country depicting how mental enhancement helps people perform better. The daughter said I had a funny personality and wanted to see what we had to offer. When her parents brought her in, they expressed that she was struggling with depression and had "tried" psychologists, psychiatry and medication. They said she has had very little success and has almost given up on therapy because it doesn't help and that she had considered taking her own life on several occasions. Inherently, I knew if I was going to work with her, my primary goal would be to connect with her and build trust before I began deploying psychological protocols and practices. As such, she began mental coaching with me and for the first three or four sessions all we did was pull out our phones and listen to each other's favorite songs. I also sang some of my favorite rap songs and even danced to the beat of my and her favorite hip-hop artists. Almost instantly, she began to smile and even laugh at my dancing skills and ability to rap. This level of emotional intimacy clearly set the foundation for me to impart several techniques that she talks about in her rap poem depicted in chapter 12; her name is

Addie L., her rap poem speaks for itself. Our ability to recognize the signs of anxiety and depression and how to help students process and regulate the perceived pressures in their lives will help us curtail anxiety, depression and yes, even suicide.

Suicide, especially here in the state of Colorado, keeps escalating. Colorado's one of the states that reports the highest suicide rate among adolescents. The underlying cause are the macro and micro ecosystems we discussed in Chapter Three. For every child that takes his or her own life, there are 10 to 15 others who are thinking about the same thing or considering taking that same action. Some people suffer quietly in the dark, there are usually clues; we just need to "see" them. We've got to understand how we are impacting our students and take time to truly connect in real life, in real time, in real ways. Our children are counting on it.

Sandy Clough on the Death of His Son, Ryan

My son Ryan took his own life back on May 4, 2017. It is a crisis of epic proportions that is impacting our youth today. It hit home for me when I personally had to walk it out with my own son. In fact, that was the day he went missing, but it turned out to be a full two weeks to the day before his body was found near the Kansas–Missouri border.

As much as I recall the agony that my wife Jean and I experienced during that time, I also remember the extraordinary support I received from our circle of friends in and around Denver. Most notably Rick, and also Scott Hastings, who offered to participate and even lead in the search for Ryan.

Rick was living and working down in Miami at the time for the Miami Dolphins. Adam Gase was the head coach, and the Dolphins were busy going through off-season training activities. Nonetheless, Adam encouraged Rick to do whatever he needed to do, even if it meant leaving work for an extended period. I will always be grateful for that and always thankful that Rick and Adam invited me down to Miami to visit and spend time with them later that autumn.

The day after Ryan had been officially declared a missing person, dozens of his friends from in and around Overland Park, Kansas began a search for him. More than anything, those men and women showed me that Ryan's impact on their lives and the lives of others had been profound – more than I could have imagined.

On the night of May 18th, the police appeared at our house right around the time we had returned from dinner with Rick's family. They had found Ryan's body a short distance from his parked car, which had been spotted the night of his disappearance. Jean and I had assumed by then that he would not be found alive, though there were always flickers of hope. I was grateful that his friends had not found his body as they searched for him 13 days earlier and that it was officials that had made the discovery.

Much of my grief centered on the many talks over the phone that Ryan and I had since he had been cited for driving under the influence on March 31st. He would tell me about feelings he had never experienced before, which I believe took a large effort to open up, to acknowledge pain, which he had previously buried. In other words, I considered this a positive development.

I had been going through a process of recovery myself, one that encouraged a rediscovery of past secrets concealed deep inside my soul. But what was working for me at more of an advanced stage did not necessarily work for Ryan. His degree of distress seemed insurmountable, so an uncovering of secrets or feelings he had never had to yet experience and process served to heighten his fear.

THE MOMENT LEADERS ARE BORN

I was left wondering if, as a father, I should have been more in touch with what he was feeling, his fear of going to court, of having his friends, co-workers, and employers "find him out." No amount of encouragement seemed sufficient to soothe him. He would soon lose his battle to these fears and end his life to escape them.

I had last seen Ryan in February when we were joined by his roommate at a Kansas basketball game, kind of an annual rite for the two of us. Ryan always had a special sense for sports, a real instinct and appreciation for what separated success from failure, both individually and collectively. It always seemed as if I learned far more from him than he ever did from me.

At his memorial service, our daughter, Sarah, Jean, and I were astonished by how many drove long distances to attend his services. We met a good many of his friends we had never even seen before during the dark days of saying goodbye to him. Through them all, I felt Ryan's presence. It helped to offer light and love. Rick spoke about our knowing "exactly where Ryan was," that he was no longer "missing," if he ever had been. It was comforting, too, hearing from an old friend, Avalanche official Jean Martineau, that I "was not alone."

Suicide, of course, carries a certain social stigma, but Jean and I always felt that it was important to be honest about it. Shading the truth would be pointless. And in fact, we never came to dread supposed punitive societal attitudes. They simply weren't there for us. But it would be less than honest to reflect and not admit to feelings of extreme regret and occasional self-loathing. Why didn't I interrupt a vacation in March down in Fort Lauderdale to go visit Ryan, as Jean had done earlier in the month? Why hadn't he fully felt my love and respect for him and not been able to find the self-love that might have shielded him from the unendurable pain of having made one mistake?

In the next few months, I came across a C.S. Lewis book entitled,

DECISION POINT

A Grief Observed. Underlined, there was a passage that read, "Part of every misery is, so to speak, the misery's shadow or reflection: the fact that you don't merely suffer but have to keep on thinking about the fact that you suffer. I not only live each endless day in grief, but live each day thinking about living each day in grief." At the same time, though, I continued to be reminded of the love and support I was receiving. Much came from Rick and my colleagues at work, as well as from others in groups I had newly joined.

I had never repudiated my faith, nor had I rejected God. However, my conscious contact was limited, along with a deeper understanding. When I thought of Ryan, on daily walks especially, I realized that I could be more than I had become, in a manner of speaking. I had grown weary of the self-flagellation, the second-guessing, and the suffering.

Gradually, I came to embrace and accept that the time and love shared with Ryan, his death, and my grief are and will forever more be a part of my life. Ryan had seen my strengths and my weaknesses, and I could hear him occasionally telling me to push ahead with my life, that there would be adventures and challenges to come. At work I found that I could be open to praise coming from listeners rather than being consumed by their very occasional criticisms.

Often in me there has lurked a feeling of having been deprived – of joy, of control, of the chance to see my son's life play out as it should have. Yet now, Rick and others from whom I closed myself off in the past have shown me that my blessings have far outweighed any real deprivation. I have been given the chance to glimpse love and a life shared with the knowledge that there is a plan out there unfolding, even if I don't always recognize it.

Through loss I have learned that, while pain is inevitable, suffering is a choice, particularly for those who have been blessed and privileged, as I have.

There is a poem from Paul-David Almond that I look at here and there, and it has helped me make sense of things:

I'll Never Really Know

I can ask, and have, a thousand times why you took yourself away
I can cry, and will, a million tears, but still it slips away.
I can rail, and have, a hundred ways at how you chose to go,
But ah, the pain which you endured, I'll never really know.

I can try, and must, to live my life, but still there seems a lack.
I can grow, and have amidst the pain, yet still keep looking back.
I can pray, and do, that through the hurt forgiveness lives to grow,
But all the times we might have touched, I'll never really know.

But all the times we might have touched, I'll never really know.
I know you never meant for things to turn out quite this way,
But the legacy you've left behind is a heavy price to pay.
If I could sum the future up, I'd say, 'Just let it go.'
But since I'm out of miracles, I'll never really know.

I can cope, and do, with memories that sometimes flood my mind.
I can laugh, and have, at all the quirks you've passed on down the line.
I can hope, and do, that through your life, my own has more to show,
But will I ever lose the pain?
I'll never really know.

Will I ever forget you?
I'll never, really… no.

∗∗∗

85

DECISION POINT

So often we talk about the word *love* or the phrase, *I love (someone)*. We will say, "I love you," or, "I'm in love with someone." It's kind of an abstract term. What does it mean? Having been around Sandy and his family for some time now, I know how much he loved Ryan and the joy he felt when watching their annual Kansas basketball game together. Jean, Sara and Sandy are very loving, giving people; so, you can image my heartbreak when I hear Sandy question his communication and behavior earlier in the chapter. As a psychologist, I am aware that most parents tend to question themselves after their child has taken their own life; however, I do know this family was very supportive and loving in Ryan's life. As a father, there are times I have regrets about something I said to my son's yesterday much less in the context of suicide. As parents, we do the best we can in the moment, with the skills we have at that moment; that has to be enough.

What does love really look like? You can't put it in your hand. Is it red? Is it green? Is it blue? Is it small? Is it big? You don't know. It's an abstract concept, love.

You just know it when you feel it. It's an attachment, if you will, on an emotional level. To be scientific, it involves the limbic system, the emotional centers of the brain. It involves the pituitary gland releasing oxytocin, which we also call the "love drug." It's all that – the science – plus the existential piece of just being attached to someone and caring about that person and expressing that care through communication and behavior; it's a deep stirring of emotion and euphoria. And that's the one thing I would like to talk about right now, how we know, feel love and express love in our society.

In my opinion, oftentimes we do not express enough love, especially to our children and our adolescents. Oftentimes we're so busy constructing and making them accountable and deploying the structure in place to help raise them that we overlook communicating this on a genuine level that they fully understand. We rarely just sit down with our children and stroke their hair or lay down on their bed and hold hands and talk about life. We don't do enough of that, making true connection. And I think it's showing in the breakdown of relationships and expressing itself in the highest suicide rates among adolescents. The suicide rate spikes between ages 14 and 21 and leaves a wide gap and opportunity for us to make a significant change. We've really got to improve in our society how we express love verbally and nonverbally and how we can really take an interest in our children's lives on a core level.

For me as I relate with my sons, I oftentimes love to hug them and kiss them on their lips and on their neck as an expression of my love for them. As they are adolescent boys and they're growing up, they oftentimes don't want to accept that, but it is how we communicate. I keep on demonstrating my love for them, and sometimes they accept it, and sometimes they resist it. I love holding hands with my sons. It's a little unusual in our culture here in the United States (US), but it's very common in Europe, Spain, Italy, and Greece to see fathers and sons holding hands in that form of expression of family love.

In the US, we delineate power distance theory; that is, we tend to exercise power and are comfortable having power over others in our life. Education, wealth, attractive appearance among other factors tend to make us feel privileged and ok with having power and distance from others. We tend to think power is exercised through behavior that is convicted and puissant; basically, the opposite of showing vulnerability. Truly, vulnerability is at the core of love. Through vulnerability, we can express love, and through love we can become vulnerable. These are key areas for adolescents' growth, to express love and be shown love in very profound and outward, tangible ways. I think the sentiments by Addie (see Chapter Twelve) on how I was able to reach her when nobody else could shows how to support that need for our young adolescents to feel love. It was as simple as taking an interest in her music, taking an interest in her, and just hanging out with her, talking, and extending personal invitations, like inviting her to my son's football games so that we were able to do things on a social level. It created connection at a core level.

We're talking about love and how to express that to our adolescents and to one another, really. Love is the answer. It reminds me of the John Ford Coley song, "Love is the Answer." It is a deep song with profound lyrics. As you listen, it touches you, but it also gives you fresh insight into a young person's pain. They just need love, like we all do. In my humble opinion, sharing that with the young adolescents in our world can go a long way in curtailing the suicide rate in our country.

One of the song's lyrics that is profound to me, says so much: "I can't stay here anymore." For me that means, "I can't stay in a place that doesn't have love anymore."

And I've looked high and low. I've been from shore to shore to shore. If there's a shortcut, I'd have surely found it, but there's no easy way around it. Light of the world, shine on me. Love is the answer.

That's a beautiful way to put it. Adults often try to find joy and happiness in careers, career titles, power, things, cars, homes, clothes, jewelry, but really after all of that, when he said he's looked from shore to shore, love is the answer. For our teens and young adults, they have learned in their short lives, "there's no easy way," and the pressure to perform is constantly driving them. Often, they feel unloved and unlovable, except when performing, and then, only when they are excelling; we have to change this.

Who knows why someday we all must die. We're all homeless boys and girls, and we are never heard. It's such a lonely, lonely, lonely world.

In many ways it is. And for an adolescent who doesn't feel accepted by peers or that they don't fit into their world or that they are unloved unless performing, and they might be in that exact moment of desperation, in the act of taking their own life, what a lonely world it is in their eyes, at that moment, right before they commit the act of taking their own life. It can't get any lonelier than that; they can't feel the love or see the hope, and they just want an avenue of escape.

. . . someday we all must die. We're all homeless boys and girls.

In essence, he's saying we're homeless, meaning we may have a home, a house, a structure that surrounds us, but is it our home? Is it full of love that we can feel and receive? Are we home? Are we in a place that we feel safe in our own skin and in our own body, at peace, and fully content?

Tell me, are we alive or just we a dying planet . . . Ask the man in your heart for the answer.

That verse really resonates with me. I love that because so many times we look for answers in so many places when maybe we should focus on the questions. The questions illuminate more critical inquiry than the answers. Oftentimes when people get answers, they relax, they stop searching, they stop inquiring and the pursuit of more. To me the most delicious part of discovery is critical inquiry, asking questions, exploring, stretching, and growing. The questions can be very profound. When he says, "Ask the man in your heart for the answer," I think that's a powerful place to look – inward; the answers are in you all along.

He has a series of statements that he makes in the middle of the song that I think are profound, as well.

And when you feel afraid, love one another. When you've lost your way, love one another. And when you're all alone, love one another. And when you're far from home, love one another. And when you're down and out, love one another. And when your hopes run out, love one another. And when you need a friend, love one another. And when you're near the end, love. We got to love. We got to love one another. Light of the world, shine on me. Love is the answer.

It's profound to me because we can search high and low from shore to shore for happiness and joy, and oftentimes we search for it in things, in homes and cars, TVs, gadgets, clothes, all those things. But at the end of the day, "ask the man in your heart for the answer." For us, it's the challenge to mentor the younger set and to get them to a place of critical thinking where they can process their feelings and thoughts and identify who they are and where they are going, and, mostly, what they need to *receive* love in this world.

LOVE IS THE ANSWER…

THE MOMENT LEADERS ARE BORN

LOVE IS THE ANSWER
England Dan & John Ford Coley, Original Artists

Name your price
A ticket to paradise
I can't stay here anymore

And I've looked high and low
I've been from shore to shore to shore
If there's a short cut
I'd have found it
But there's no easy way around it

Light of the world
Shine on me
Love is the answer
Shine on us all
Set us free
Love is the answer

. . .LOVE IS THE ANSWER. . .

I want to share another special person to me that involves Love: Coach Jacobs. Coach Jacobs (Coach Jake) is one of the best teachers of the game of football I have ever encountered. He taught footwork and technique better than any coach I have ever been around at any level, including the NFL. Beyond that, he taught leadership and communication skills and how to be accountable and responsible in everyday life.

There were times when he took an hour out of his day to just teach me about being a responsible human being. To this day, he is a major spoke in the wheel of my leadership and performance paradigm. I love Coach Jake.

DECISION POINT

His daughter, Mollie, meant the world to him and the Jacobs family. Mollie's youth was marked with great displays of love and compassion for others. She had great depth for a young person. From a young age Mollie knew her mission was music and the arts. She was able to play the piano by ear and composed her first song at the age of 5 years old. She wrote poems, and the most memorable one was written when she was just 11 years young. This poem, "The Sunset," was submitted for a Superintendent Award.

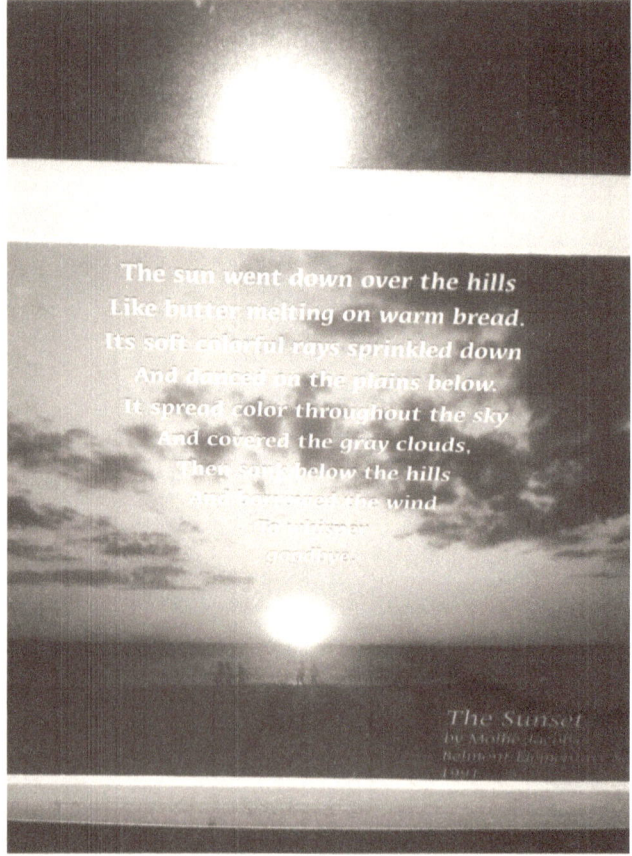

The sun went down over the hills
Like butter melting on warm bread.
Its soft colorful rays sprinkled down
And danced on the plains below.
It spread color throughout the sky
And covered the gray clouds.
Then sank below the hills
And calmed the wind

The Sunset
by Mollie Jacobs
Belmont Elementary
1997

"The Sunset" by Mollie Jacobs, 11

THE MOMENT LEADERS ARE BORN

Music was a part of her soul. She would eventually pursue her love of music in New York at the SUNY Purchase College. She also had a keen connection to people and compassion for everyone she met. On Sundays, she would extend herself to talk with all the grandmas and grandpas at church, even when she was just three years old. She touched one older gentleman when she made him a "Get Well" card. He was so moved because he did not have children or grandchildren of his own. She brought joy wherever she went. She could communicate easily with the young and the old. Her dog, Rocky, was her best buddy. She had a great sense of humor that was infectious and made many laugh.

It is so difficult to imagine this precious soul, full of light and hope and love, would make such a turn around and fall into a place of depression. She went off to New York full of hope but returned to Pueblo, Colorado to address her depression and misuse of alcohol.

Sadly, it was a car accident on January 13, 2002, at 3:30 in the morning, that would take her life. "Only the Good Die Young," resonates with those who knew her. On Sunday, January 13, 2002, I called out to God to let me know she was at home with Christ. On Monday, January 14, 2002, I received a call from my friends, Tom and Annie, who are like family. Annie shared a vivid dream she had of Mollie, riding on a white winged horse against a bright blue sky. She was riding towards the light. It brought great peace to us all. Who says God doesn't answer prayers?

No, time does not heal the pain. Time doesn't help answer the question, "Why?" Time doesn't bring answers like, "Why her, God?" or "Why such a young and vibrant gal?" However, time does make me thankful for the treasure of time once spent together and for the way she touched so many lives. Time allows me to savor the talents she displayed, her humor, memories of her smile, and mostly, her mighty spirit that lives on.

DECISION POINT

Mollie Ann Jacobs
June 25, 1980 – January 13, 2002

STAIRWAY TO HEAVEN

"My plans are not your plans, nor are my ways your ways, says the Lord! Just as the heavens are higher than the earth, so are my ways higher than your ways and my thoughts than your thoughts."

—Isaiah 55:8–10 (New International Version, NIV)

Chapter Seven

HUMILITY TRANSFORMS INTO BEAUTY

The world is full of shiny lights, the allure of success, wealth, power, and position; people are driven to pursue dreams and success, and as quick as blowing out a flaming match, it can all be snuffed out. What is left is what truly matters. You can work hard, dream big, sacrifice to make it all a reality, give up free time and holidays, family time and vacation days, and finally see reward. And in an instance, a curveball can fly out of left field and wipe it all out. What is left is what truly matters. Beauty, true beauty from within, forged from the fire of this life experience is what is revealed. Through humility, surrender, acceptance, and a whole lot of grit and grace, true beauty evolves; an ataraxy, if you will.

This was the experience of my amazing friend Sharla (Shar) Manglitz as she went from a high performing, high-powered litigator to a vulnerable woman in the battle of her life, facing double mastectomy and fighting for her life through breast cancer. Shar, as I call her, is a great friend and an exquisite human being, and I was able to watch from the sidelines as she faced her battle and emerge victoriously as a beautiful human being.

THE MOMENT LEADERS ARE BORN

We were meant to be friends, best friends in many ways. We have been there for each other for the last several years through many of life's difficult moments. We met a few years ago, when my good friend Julius Thomas and I went to a networking event in Fort Lauderdale. I also invited another friend of mine, Carlos Alonso (whose brother, Kiko Alonso, played for the Dolphins and now is a starting linebacker for the New Orleans Saints). The three of us – Carlos, Julius, and myself – had just arrived at this networking event for attorneys. I had been invited by another attorney friend, and I was scanning the room to find her.

Instead, this beautiful woman came into my view. I mean, she was strikingly beautiful – tall, maybe six-foot-tall, beautiful blonde hair. She was elegance in motion, if you will. The attorney who had invited me to the networking event was engaged in a lively conversation with this striking woman who had just caught my eye. We approached the small group to say thank you for the invitation, and my attorney friend introduced me to Shar. We shook hands as my attorney friend introduced us, "Rick is the psychologist for the Miami Dolphins. I just wanted you to meet him." I greeted her warmly and turned to introduce her to Julius and Carlos. We had a short conversation about the event and our respective fields of work.

Later in the evening, the networking event turned more social, and as the music began to play, people stayed and danced. We stayed and had a good time for a while and danced the night away. Then, as I would later learn, Shar sent me an email the next day, but I never saw it. It must have been delivered to my junk email, and I never received it.

Time marched on, and Shar and I had no further communication. Fast forward to May of 2018, and I was back in California for a very grave situation. Unfortunately, my best male friend, Bobby Major, who I'll discuss further in Chapter Eight, was very sick with colon cancer. He had beat it once, but it returned, and he was battling a second bout of the deadly cancer. It quickly progressed from its onset in March until May, and now, it seemed like just a matter of time until it was terminal. I was traveling back and forth between Colorado and the Bay Area, where Bobby lived, to see him and visit with him and his wife, Juenko. We (Juenko) and I talked about how we were going to celebrate his life when the time came and how she would reach me in the last 72 hours of his life. He passed away on the 11th of May 2018.

It was a very, very challenging time for me. As I made my way to the airport to fly back home to Denver after he passed, I was sobbing. I was very emotional at losing my best friend. We were best friends for 34 years. It was very challenging for me and still is to this day. As I went through security at the airport and walked to my departure gate, I sat down in a small restaurant and ordered a sandwich and a glass of wine. As I sat down, intending to eat my sandwich, I started to cry and sob again because of the enormous loss of my best friend Bobby Major.

As I sat there, it didn't really matter to me who saw me crying. I was just going to express my emotions and was fairly oblivious of anyone around me, anyway. This gentleman approached me and put his hand on my shoulder. He looked at me and asked, "Man, Bro, are you okay?" I looked at him and said, "No, I'm not. I'm really not okay. I just lost my best friend; he just passed away."

The man offered a lot of compassion and said, "Oh man. I'm really sorry about that. Do you mind if I sit down and talk to you?" I was like, "Cool. You're good, Man. Good." And so, he did. We sat there and connected while he simply listened to me as I shared my pain.

Most people would say he was a stranger, but I would say that it was destiny that he was there and made himself available when I needed someone the most. We talked for the next hour about the loss of my friend. Then we talked about him, about his career as a minor league baseball coach and just really shared a lot. He was very, very in-touch with his feelings, very present in his emotions, and he really supported me through that hour before I caught my flight. His name is Adam, but I call him Brosy. He calls me Brosy, like brothers. He lives in Santa Cruz, California. But that day, our paths were meant to cross at that airport at that moment.

We exchanged numbers and stayed in touch over the next several months. One night, I was in Denver staying with my father when I got a phone call late at night from Brosy. It wasn't uncommon for him to call me late at night when he had a break because, on the weekends, to make extra money, he would serve as a bartender at a local hotel and worked late hours. So, I got this phone call approximately 11:00 p.m., Mountain Standard Time, knowing it's his 10:00 p.m. Pacific Coast Time.

I answer the phone and he ask's, "Brosy, whats up?"

"I'm good, Man," I say, glad to hear his friendly voice. "I'm just ready to go to sleep, Bro."

He seemed surprised. "Wow," he said. "Okay. Before you go, do you know someone named Sharla?"

By this time, several months had passed since I had met Shar over a year ago at the networking event, so my first response was, "No. No, not by name."

But he persisted, "Bro, you should know who this girl is. She's beautiful." He began to describe her, "She's real tall. She's blonde. She knows you."

It didn't trigger anything at first, "Interesting. How does she know me?"

"She met you at a networking event in Fort Lauderdale. She's an attorney."

"Oh, yes. Okay. I remember. I remember who she is." And before I could put all the pieces together in my mind, he had already put her on the phone. We proceeded to talk for the next hour; it was surreal.

"Hey, Dr. P. How you been?" she greeted me from the other end of the phone.

I immediately started with a smile, hearing her strong, warm voice. "Good, good; please call me Rick. It's been a long time," I said.

"Yeah. Did you ever get my email?" she asked rather quizzically. "I emailed you the next day after I met you."

"I did not," I said as my mind whirled through my inbox. *How could I have missed that?*

"Oh, wow. Okay," she said, sounding somewhat disappointed but hard to read.

Now I'm curious what the email said.

We talked, and she informed me that she was in Santa Cruz, California because she was visiting her sister who lived there. She was staying at a hotel and had just decided to go get a glass of wine down at the hotel bar, when she met Adam, AKA "Brosy"

Here's where it gets interesting. When Shar went down to the bar, she sat down, and Adam was serving. It's a really small bar, and I happen to know because I have been there myself on a previous trip. There are only maybe five places to sit. Sharla was sitting at one of those little tables, having a drink, and Brosy was talking to another patron about me, but he didn't mention me by name.

What Adam said to the patron was, "Yeah, Man, I met this dude at the airport, and he was crying. So I walked up to him and just said, 'Bro, you okay?' And he said, 'No, Man. I just lost my best friend.' " Adam was explaining, "Man, this guy was really vulnerable. He was open. He didn't care who saw him cry or anything. He was just really, really present and in the moment expressing that."

Shar perked up, not believing her ears. How could she be sitting at a hotel bar in California and overhearing this story. *I know it's gotta be him; that's no coincidence.*

"I introduced myself, and I talked to him, and we ended up talking for an hour. This dude's really cool, Man. He's, like, a sports psychologist and works with pro teams, and he helps people. We had a lot to talk about while he was waiting for his plane."

Sharla, sitting on the other end of the bar, looked at the guest at the bar and then over to Adam and smiled as she said, "I know who you're talking about."

He looked at her and her half-empty wine glass and asked, "Who? What do you mean? Do you know who I'm talking about?"

She smiled wryly, "You're describing that psychologist. I know who you're talking about."

"Who?" he asked defiantly, as if she was pulling his leg and testing him.

"Dr. P," she said, certain of herself.

He stopped talking, both hands on his hips in disbelief. "How did you know?"

"Through your description. He's cool. He's funny. He's smart. He's dynamic. He's vulnerable. I knew that about him the moment I met him, that there was something very different about this guy, and that's who it is," she said with a smirk again.

That's when Brosy decided to call me and ask, "Do you know Sharla?"

So, from Fort Lauderdale, Florida to Santa Cruz, California to Denver, Colorado, our meeting was meant to be. Shar and I now had a connection. We stayed in touch following that phone call, and every time I visited Fort Lauderdale, we would get together. We'd have lunch or dinner and hang out. Shar has a son, nine years old, named Dante. And I have a daughter named Dante. We started to see how many things we had in common. She was an attorney. I was a psychologist. We were both highly educated with very open minds. It helped us to connect as friends from the get-go.

Another time we learned we had a connection point was when I was sharing a story with her, "I went to the coolest party that I may have ever gone to at this high-rise in Harbor Beach in Fort Lauderdale. They had this Motown band playing and people were dancing by the pool from two years old to 92. I've never been at a party where you had that age range and the diversity at this party." I said, "It was so much more fun that the band was from Motown. We had a great time."

"What was the name of that high-rise?" she asked with more curiosity.

"I don't really remember. I think it was called Avenue of the Americas or something of the Americas Towers." I was trying to remember.

The next thing stunned us both. "I was at that party in May or in March, but it was in 2018," she said excitedly.

"Oh my gosh. Wow!"

We were destined to meet even before we did at the networking event. It was such a beautiful story unfolding in new ways every time we spoke. The way Shar and I met was destiny. The universe brought us together not once but twice.

And with that foundation of friendship, I choose to stand by her side as she battles her breast cancer and is now undergoing her second round of breast cancer treatment. She had surgery in December of 2019 and presently is getting chemotherapy. Before Shar had breast cancer, she was a litigator in Fort Lauderdale and Miami was very successful. With everything going for her, including her beauty and charisma, her intelligence, and her success, she really had the world in the palm of her hands, or so it would seem.

She was a powerful presence in South Florida. In addition to her work as a litigator, she also worked as a runway and photography still model. Then the destructive force of breast cancer struck. As a result, she underwent a double mastectomy, followed by years of recovery.

While the epitome of strength, with a fierce spirit, with great vulnerability, she expressed to me that she went "from model to mutilated." She has had to learn to face it like a fighter. She has had to employ some of her courtroom tactics to employ critical thinking and tenacity and to identify the true culprit of her good health. She has transitioned to a new form of beauty as a bedside fighter, no longer the powerful courtroom litigator that she once was.

And through this, she has learned a new way of facing life with humility. She has had to challenge her negative thoughts and intentionally choose a strong, positive mindset. There is great beauty in every trial she has faced. She has learned a new way to think and process and project herself. I have seen her begin to bloom in a new way through this process.

Cancer is considered a bad thing, especially in America; it is seen as a strike of misfortune. But in Shar's case, I choose to see it from another perspective. I think that, because of the cancer, she is more beautiful than ever. She's always had beauty on the outside; that's unmistakable. But her beauty on the inside has illuminated, offering a new dimension of beauty about her. This wellspring of beauty erupted because of the immense challenges she has faced and overcome through her battle with breast cancer and the process of recovery.

Shar defaulted to showing her beauty on the outside because this is what society valued in her. A model who's six feet tall, check. A model who's blonde and beautiful, check. Smart, articulate, graceful – all those things played to her advantage as a successful litigator. But through this challenge, this tragedy, this trauma of breast cancer and the double mastectomy came her inner strength and the beauty within. It revealed the beauty within that she always knew was there but didn't necessarily postulate because she had been rewarded so handsomely for her external beauty her whole life. From power litigator to bedside fighter, she was fighting for her life and her esteem and self-concept. But through that storm, it created an opportunity for immense beauty to emerge.

Shar and I were destined to become best friends. Many people look at her and look at me and ask why we don't date, but that has never been on the table. "We just never have had that attraction from day one," I have always responded. "It's been more about supporting each other as friends." We always thought of each other as just friends and that we were here to love and support each other through the journey of life.

She shared with me how her life since the cancer was now defined in new ways, like finding beauty in the smallest things: the smell of flowers, the sounds of nature, the surf crashing against the beach, the laughter of friendship, our friendship together, how she would fly to Colorado at the drop of a dime if I needed her and I would fly to Florida, at the drop of the dime if she needed me. She's been back to Colorado multiple times to support me through funerals of my friends and for my father's funeral. I've been to Florida, most recently, to support her through her yet another breast cancer surgery.

THE MOMENT LEADERS ARE BORN

Shar has shared that if she had not contracted cancer, she may still be that fierce litigator that's just running through life, like a knife through butter, through the world, not noticing the small things like the smell of the flowers. This struggle illuminated the beauty of life around her and revealed the internal, intrinsic beauty of Sharla Manglitz.

Life is not defined by titles, runway modeling gigs, power litigating, or wealth; it's defined by the beauty we have within. Her internal beauty transcended the cancer she could not defeat on her own. Through this, she is a great example of self-transcendence because she had to shift the focus from herself and her law career to helping others. She found value and meaning in kindness. She was able to extrapolate from the horror of cancer into the beauty of simple love, joy, and laughter. She began to come out from behind her legal shield and become more playful, sharing good deeds with others and showing support and love to me in many profound ways. She accepted my friendship unconditionally. She became friends with people involved in my life, supported them, and loved them unconditionally. And we have had so much fun as friends.

Essentially, what Shar has done as she has transformed through this process is produced fruit in others' lives as well as her own. She has elevated the emotions of herself, rediscovered her true self, and connected with the world around her. All of this has been engaging to watch and be a part of. The awe is hard to fully express, the amazement of the simplicity of this beautiful process and the beautiful being it continues to reveal has brought new life from the darkness of his battle. There is truly beauty from the ashes, and if you change your lens, the way you view things, you can see it unfold before your eyes. Shar is a testimony of true leadership that is exposed when life throws curveballs and champions are faced with fire; they are forged mightier than ever before.

Another Testimony of Women Winning as Champions of Their Life

Megan Mulqueen on Reaching out to Dr. P for Mindset Reprogramming to Become a Champion in Equestrian Competitions

Before I begin, I want to assert that I have often said I have zero self-esteem. To me this was always a normal, typical thing to say. But after I met Dr. P, I realized I needed to reframe my word choice. He breaks it up into colored boxes: Red, yellow, and green. These boxes take on the traffic signal meanings that we often recognize as stop, go, and slowly with caution. Saying that I have zero self-esteem was clearly red-box propaganda, not green-box rhetoric that he expects from his clients. You see, Dr. P expects you to choose your words very carefully to prepare the brain for success, as he calls it. So, not only has he helped me with my performance wants and needs, he has also taught me to address my self-concept and self-esteem needs concurrently. He has taught me how to examine my ecosystems, both micro and macro, that influence my belief systems. That is, who am I hanging around and how do they grow me? This framework led to me gaining some relationships and losing some relationships. Overall, I continue to grow and learn that I have complete control over how I think, feel, behave, and perform. It's such a beautiful place to be.

I met Dr. Perea in a most unusual way, while sitting on a horse! It was a likely place, as I am an equestrian, but unlikely that I would act on my decision to call him while I was mounted on my horse.

I am a competitive person by nature, always striving to be the best that I can be at whatever task is before me. I am also very sports-oriented, and in recent years, I have enjoyed the equestrian sport of reining. It is an adrenaline rush and is surprisingly harder than it looks!

My riding coach has repeatedly said to me that my biggest obstacles are in my mind. I have the skills to be a great competitor, but I need to believe that I can succeed at competing. I knew I would need help addressing these mindsets in the arena.

Over the past couple of years, I have seen Dr. Perea on TV and heard him on the radio, and his insights intrigued me. I scoured the Internet and social media looking for clues to his background and for tidbits of advice that could help me in any way. Finally, I decided to reach out to him, explain my situation and my thoughts about what I was looking to achieve, and ask whether he could help me.

I looked him up and, with a strong determination in the moment, called him while sitting on my horse! Dr P. called me right back, and from that moment, I knew I had done the right thing. During our first brief phone call, he made me feel relaxed and comfortable, and he made it obvious that he was listening to my every word. By the second phone call, he was already pointing out to me how I was communicating and how I could reformat my thoughts to be more productive and positive.

These were very powerful experiences. I was very impressed with his insight, and I relayed the results of our conversation to my riding coach, who was very excited for me. I made an office appointment and the rest is history.

After a couple of visits with Dr. P, I started sharing my story with my friends and family as I helped them reformat their interactions with me. My riding coach and his assistants were very good about integrating the new concepts and challenging me to restructure my mindset. The first few competitions that I went to after I started my program with Dr. P were learning situations where I pondered how I felt and how I dealt with challenges. My goal was, and still is, to maintain positive habits and behaviors. I am learning to deal with circumstances and people beyond my control and to influence those situations and to identify people who I can help – even in everyday life.

Ultimately, my experience with ThinkOne, Dr. P's organization, is about growing and fortifying my mental toughness and happiness. In competition, there are always things I can improve upon for next time. Overall, I am learning, and sometimes relearning, how to deal with challenges, and it shows in my successes in competition as well as in my overall satisfaction in life. I am pleased to say that through my work with Dr.P, I most recently won every event I entered at one of the most competitive events nationally.

Dr. P Opines Regarding Gender Responsiveness and Equity

While I feel that Megan's account of how self-concept and self-esteem are unique to her and my applications for her, it is not a secret that women in our society and culture tend to have a different level of expectations for themselves in general than their male counterparts. A case in point is when I was a college professor at The University of Colorado in Denver, I would observe women comport themselves in a fashion that generally was quite different from my male students. For example, after class was over for the day, when males would approach me, they would, in general, walk up to me and keep their shoulders square and make consistent eye contact while speaking to me. Conversely, most women when approaching me to begin a conversation, in general, would "slide" from a 45° angle so they would not be forced to see me "head-on." This more passive approach is consistent with the research that women tend to have, in general, a lower expectation for themselves when it comes to occupational and educational performance.

To me, this is sad and disappointing; it's sad in that, women to this day still only make 78 cents on the dollar as compared to their male counterparts. However, this is a symptom of a general lower performance expectation set into motion by the primary ecosystems that little girls, who later become women, are exposed to early in their lives. As men and fathers, we must instill in our women, and daughters, a sense of strong self-concept that will foster a level of high expectations to actualize and transcend themselves when it comes to occupational and performance objectives, goals, and expectations.

It's disappointing in that, in American culture, many men do not necessarily champion women to have equity in our society; unfortunately, many men still see women as playing a supporting, even subservient, role in the family structure and in occupations in general. If we are ever going to close the gender wage gap that has existed since data had been recorded, we as males must uphold our females in an equitable fashion that praises their unique skillsets. Although women have a role, in this elevation, it is men and only men that can elevate women from a didactical position. That is, we as men must seek learning opportunities from women and reframe the situation so that it is understood that women have an eclectic skill set that is valued and has meaning in our lives. We need to honor and elevate that belief until it is more widespread. We I first heard Megan say she "had zero self-esteem," it got my attention. For her to make such an assertion was both sad and culturally driven. First, Megan is an insightful, smart, dynamic person who has so much to offer the world. In my opinion, she was merely repeating a deficit-based rendition that is overtly and primarily covertly communicated in our media, especially social media, every day. The great news is Megan now knows what I knew before she recognized it in herself: She is an amazing person who is only limited by her purposeful thoughts. In other words, she shapes her thoughts, so her thoughts don't shape her. She is a great example of how we can go from a deficit thinker to an asset thinker by merely re-shaping our thoughts through our techniques and protocols.

Another germane example of how women possess a highly valued skill that is somewhat unique to women is in leadership – more specifically, relational leadership. According to *The Bass Handbook of Leadership* (2008), women tend to possess a relational strength to leadership, while their male counterparts generally are strong in the task orientation of leadership. Better yet, androgynous leadership, which possesses both relational and task orientation, is the most effective type of leadership today, according to Bass. This makes a great deal of sense when one considers a person's learning styles – that people learn from different senses like visual, auditory, and tactile, to name a few. Further, in a study conducted with 144 undergraduate students, Bass (2012) asserts that women tend to be more effective in supervisory and leadership roles. For example, when the students were broken into groups, the groups that were led by women as compared to men were not only more productive but also more creative and innovative. Further, Bass postulates that, when profiling 50 of the top Fortune 100 companies, women tend to be stronger on such performance factors as communicating, planning, controlling, leading, problem solving, and managing relationships. It is important to also recognize that it seems androgynous leadership, that is, leadership that possesses both task and relational orientations, tends to be the most effective leadership approach, delivered by male or female. With this research, it supports a woman's ability to lead and a gap that men can step in to fill to provide equity in the organizational context. As men, we can only learn and expand our schemata when observing women in leadership roles.

Chapter Eight

44 FOREVER

See a penny, find a penny, pick up a penny, and put it in your pocket. Many of us believe finding a penny is a sign from someone in heaven. Red birds are another such symbol; somehow if you see one, you start to see a purposeful pattern of bright red cardinals. Numbers are another one. Ever look at a clock randomly throughout the day and soon you are seeing that same number everywhere? Numbers mean something to me. I find meaning in a lot of things that show up in my life, but numbers are especially relevant to me.

Take the number "44" – it has a significant meaning in my life for many reasons. It was my football jersey number in high school, my jersey number in college, and the number of sacks I got as a defensive end/outside linebacker in my college career. I could have never intentionally gotten 44 sacks. It just never would've worked. I would have probably been too high, too low. But as it turns out, that was the number of sacks that I would have in my college football career. As it would turn out in the future, the number would again show up in a significant way.

So, 44 forever lives on because of my great friendship with Bobby Major. Our relationship spanned 34 years before he passed away of cancer. Coincidentally, his number was 44 at all three levels of football that he played. We spent many years together as friends, playing football together, just doing life together.

THE MOMENT LEADERS ARE BORN

We met one day while working out at Gold's Gym. After my football career came to an end, I acted in approximately 10 television commercials and even a TV series. I had just filmed a McDonalds television commercial, and it was airing locally. Bobby came up to me one day in the gym and asked, "Aren't you the guy in that McDonald's commercial?"

"I am," I said. "That's me."

"Wow!" he exclaimed. "Yeah, I saw you in that commercial the other day, and I said, 'Man, I know that guy.'"

That was the beginning of our friendship. We talked on a more regular basis when we'd see each other at the gym after that. He was a very kind person, I could tell – very reflective during our conversations and a great listener. It's pretty rare to come across those communication traits in a male. A lot of times males are just talking about themselves and their accomplishments, especially when you meet people at the gym. Everybody's kind of measuring themselves against one another, if you will.

Bobby and I continued to talk in the gym, and then one day I casually suggested, "We ought to go to lunch, because we're always talking in the gym and it takes away from your workout, takes me away from my workout, and it would be really good if we just have some time to talk more."

"Wow, are you serious?" he seemed taken by surprise.

"Yeah, I'd love to do that." I thought it would be great to invest more time in developing a friendship outside the gym.

"Wow, that would be great," he said.

"You seem surprised," I said.

"You know, Rick," he said, opening up, "I'm surprised by this whole relationship. For you to take the time to hang out with me— I mean, you're a former NFL guy and you make TV commercials, and you want to have lunch and invest your time in me? That's really cool." He was very humble from the beginning. But we're just two guys hanging out at the gym and doing our workouts and taking care of our health. We have great conversations, so why not spend time making new friends?

As our relationship continued to grow, he shared that he, too, had a few relationships in his life where he was experiencing a lot of ups and downs. For example, he was married, had two children, Trey and Jonte, and then went through a divorce. These trials by fire, again, forged an ironclad relationship that drew us closer together. Bobby also lost a sister to cancer years before, so he, too, knew loss of a sibling, much like me and others chronicled in this book.

He supported me through the challenges that I had while married and then while going through divorce and through my experience of being a father to my oldest daughter, Dante. We grew to be good buddies both in and outside the gym. I became the godfather of his son, Trey. He became very involved in my life and, eventually, my best male friend.

Because the number 44 had so much significance in his life and also in my life, and that occurred over 1,200 miles away in Chicago where he was born and raised, we were living these simultaneous lives in which 44 played an important role. I didn't really know the significance until he became very sick with cancer and there was a series of events that happened in which the number 44 just kept emerging and popping up in the strangest places. For example, when I went out to see him when he had first contracted cancer, the hospital room that he was in was 444, and when I came into his room, I looked at him, and I teased, "Come on, Dawg, did you choose this room because of the number?"

"No, Man. Straight up didn't do it," he mustered a smile and was as surprised, but not really, as I.

"Wow, that's a unique coincidence."

And that would start to trigger how often I would see 44. I started noticing it on license plates, in events, tickets that I would get – all randomly numbered 44. I took my sons on a trip to New York, and we took the circle line tour, and it was $44 per ticket. We kept seeing the number 44 appear. He was a great friend, and this number kept showing up to remind me of our friendship.

He would eventually pass away in May of 2018. His wife, Juenko, and I had a plan that, 72 hours before they anticipated his final days, she would call me, and I would jet out and spend the last few days with him in the Bay Area. The plan worked. I was able to do that, and during my time with him, I was able to place a bracelet I purchased just for him on his wrist, to symbolize our friendship. He was able to wear it in his last 48 hours. I wear it to this day, and I will never take it off. It's our bond; it's our bond forever.

That trip, those last 48 hours spent with him, were very challenging, excruciating, especially after he passed away. Even during my trip from Colorado to go see him on that final trip, the number 44 kept popping up. I purchased a few gifts in the gift shop, some snack food for his kids, Trey and Jontae, and a meal for myself, and the total came to $44.44. At this point, I started to look around, wondering, "How is this happening? Why is this happening? What's the significance?"

So, at the urging of one of my friends, who asked, "Have you ever looked it up on the Internet? Maybe it has some meaning," I did, and it indicated that the number 44 is a reflection of angels watching over you. At this point I began to realize there's something special here about 44 because it was such a significant number in my life and in Bobby's, and now it had become a significant number in our relationship together, even through his cancer. It happened several other times, too. When I was catching a flight after he did pass, the gate that I left out of at the San Francisco airport was 44. Upon leaving from yet another trip, we went to a pizza place, where you receive a table number, and that number was 44.

So, with all this confirmation and the significance of this double digit, I decided to get the number "44" tattooed on my arm. It will forever be there as a reminder of "44 forever" – my relationship with Bobby, my best friend, my DAWG!

Our relationship was so powerful that it also overflowed to my family. He was a great example of being a great father; it was very important to him. I used to watch Bobby as a father to Trey and to Jontae, and he was simply amazing. He was calm, he was cool, and he was collected. He would talk with them and reflect with them on many topics. I would watch from afar and just think, *Wow, I want to be a father like that.* Ironically, he would often tell me that he watched me parent my daughter and then later my sons and say, "Wow, you really have a cool relationship with your sons. Like, you're a father, just real. They respect you. They have structure and discipline in their lives, but you also just hang out with them. You can talk smack with them. You can laugh with them, chill with them. It's really cool to watch."

I think there was such a mutual respect in our relationship that we reached a level of friendship that's rarely reached in terms of emotional and psychological intimacy and vulnerability between male friends. I will forever be indebted to Bobby because of the kind and communicative human being that he was. He was a great role model and a giver. As an African American male, Bobby was different; he thrived on being authentic and vulnerable. He would open his heart and his soul; he would open his wallet to complete strangers. As a psychologist in the NFL, I can say this isn't always typical. Sometimes, this can be perceived as a sign of weakness, culturally speaking, but it never deterred Bobby. Bobby was different. He had the most innocent and beautiful smile that, if we were talking to someone, he would be open to supporting them and say, "Hey, Man, it's going to be okay, Bro." When somebody was down and out, Bobby always had a good word to add, a good nugget to contribute, and I still respect him for that.

The most important thing Bobby and I shared was the spirituality between us and all that 44 represented to us. 44 NEVER dies. It lives forever in this book, on my arm, and in our memories, forever. My tribute is to Bobby Major, the best male friend that I've ever had, the kindest person, the most vulnerable person in terms of a male that I've ever met in my life. He was a man who loved. He loved people; he loved his kids – he loved nothing more than his kids.

His famous opening two phrases were, "You know, Man," or, "Rick, I'll tell you what, Man," and that's how he would open every sentence. I sometimes reflect with Bobby to this day, and I sense he still has my back, saying, "Bro, keep going. Keep doing it, Man. Keep being a great father, a great psychologist, Dawg!"

Slowing down my travel to be focused as a great father was one of my best decisions. Bobby helped fuel that choice. That's my number one goal – to be a great father, just like Bobby. It also goes back to my dad, the role model that he was to me. My dad always put family first, always, 100%, until the day he died. I had great role models in my life; men who loved well, who truly loved, not men who like or men who, as adults, just say to their kids, "Hey, son/daughter, I support you," but men who actually loved their kids and showed it and expressed it verbally, vocally, and nonverbally.

To be better fathers, us men have to get better at being vulnerable with our kids. We adult men have to get better at being vulnerable with our sons and with our daughters and at showing them that vulnerability is a strength. It's an openness. It's being mindful. It's being emotionally intelligent. But more than anything, it's leaving your comfort zone to show them we genuinely care and can express love for them.

One of my greatest goals and objectives is to be a leader as a father. Fathers are leaders inherently, but great leaders are vulnerable, and sometimes we must push ourselves to show up in this capacity, though sometimes it may be uncomfortable. Great fathers are great leaders in terms of vulnerability, communicating, love, and showing trust.

Bobby was special, and he was my "44 Forever," but if you look at this as a certain spot for someone who was a level up from special, there's another man that would fit under the "44 Forever" category, and that is my college defensive coordinator, Coach Bill Jacobs, who I call Coach Jake and mentioned earlier in chapter 6. I think about how much he talks about his children and how much he talks about how much he's learning now as a grandfather. He's another man who loves his kids, and now granddaughter, as well. He took a loving to me when I was in college as an athlete by sitting down and talking with me about caring enough to be on time, caring enough to hand in my work so I would excel academically, and doing all the work I was supposed to do – about keeping commitments and accountability.

Bobby, my dad, coach Jake and coach Tarver (high school coach) – they all fit in this category. I'd like to think I live up to that, too. Men who truly love and are willing to show their vulnerability, willing to show that it's a strength as opposed to what many people perceive as a weakness in our society. We must always transcend ourselves as men who love others, as well as ourselves, and who show love to others and put their needs ahead of ourselves. That's what great men do. That's what my dad taught me.

Because my dad was willing to sacrifice his goals for the goals of his family, our family tree was able to change in one generation, from a farmer with a third-grade education to doctoral-level education. My dad showed my family, and specifically me, love, and there was great fruit from that; now I pass it on to my children.

These men are my role models, they showed love, gave love, and were love, and they've influenced me in great ways, and through their legacy, I now pass this on to my sons.

There is another way of love, not just through loving, but through giving generously, through being open-hearted. In our society, sometimes this plays out in the form of money, though it's not about the money at all. Giving generously and unconditionally through the tool of money can be a form of love when it is given from a pure heart. My dad showed me how to give from my heart and of everything I had. When you work your butt off for your job/career/occupation and you put everything you have into your work, like I do and like my dad did, and that hard-earned money is given to others as a support system because you care and love those people, that's true love. It's never about the money or the love of money, but about knowing that the love that motivates you to provide and give is also the motivator to produce the harvest of money to be shared.

I most recently was able to help a family bury their child of only 20 years old. They couldn't afford to do it any other way, and so I stepped up and helped that family with the gift of money that enabled them to do this; that was given in love, through the tool of money. I had the resources to do it. Perhaps someday I won't be in such a position, but having it and seeing a need, addressing it without hesitation, is a true expression of love that comes from the heart.

DECISION POINT

To meet someone else's need, especially when they would have no other way to help themselves, and to give that away unconditionally is a pure form of love. I would do it all over again.

A final example of pure love for himself and his family is Coach Larry Tarver. Coach Tarver (Coach T), was my high school defensive coach; he believed in me when even I had self-doubts. Coach T was also my biology teacher during third period in my sophomore year. One day he pulled me aside and said, "Son, we need to talk after class." I anticipated the discussion would have everything to do with football or the like. However, our conversation lasted approximately one hour, as he had an "off" period that day, and he requested a pass so I could miss my fourth period class. That hour changed the course of my high school football career and my academic expectations. Coach T said, "Richard, you have a tremendous amount of potential as a football player; in fact, I think you have a future in it if you learn to prioritize your objectives." He continued, "You have been late to my class several times this semester, and *I* am your football coach. I can only imagine what you are doing in your other classes. Further, you are very smart and can-do way better than the grade of C that you have in my class. If you stop chasing the girls, or letting them chase you, you will be a tremendous success at this school." After that meeting, I kept replaying in my mind his words and how I valued how he had taken his time, school time, to talk to me about my career, my life, and my future. That talk would change me forever – not that day, but the wheels were put into motion that day.

Coach T and his family – son, daughter, and wife – were involved in a horrific car accident that left his beautiful wife critically injured in my junior year of high school. Although the other three T's (Coach T had the moniker "Four T's" on his license plate) fully recovered from the accident, his beautiful bride sustained severe brain injuries that required several surgeries that left her needing to relearn how to walk and talk again.

Prior to the accident, she was strikingly beautiful; in fact, I always had said that if she wanted to be a model she could – she was that attractive. What I would come to learn is that she was even more beautiful on the inside, as I would often see her when I would visit Coach T when he became a head coach at another rival high school. Coach T had an interesting draw, so much so that, even though my high school was called George Washington (GW) High School, during my college and brief pro career I would always go see Coach T at his new home, called East High School. I didn't go back to GW until Coach Steve Finesilver – now an administrator at the school – reached out to me and told me that I was fortunate enough to be inducted into the school's hall of fame several years ago.

I love Coach Tarver; he modeled love for himself by having high expectations as a teacher and a coach. He modeled love for his family when he stood by them through the emotional trauma of a car accident that required years of recovery, rehabilitation, and no doubt emotional and psychological frustrations. I will forever be indebted to Coach T, not only for "the talk" back in high school, but his example of excellence in all he did as a teacher, coach and especially as a father.

Chapter Nine

NEVER HUNT ALONE

"Never hunt alone" is a football terminology on defense, and it refers to a swarming technique. Coaches have said to never hunt alone because, when you hunt alone you don't have the power of the pack. The "power of the pack" refers to the multiple talents in the pack, or those on your team. You have multiple competencies and acumens on your side when you are part of a pack, and that's powerful. You have multiple strengths that can compensate for any blind spots.

The same holds true for life; there is power in the pack – your tribe, your people, your clan, those with whom you do life. I surround myself with a strong ecosystem and am honored to have friends who have got my back. There are many challenging issues and events in life; friends help support through the pain and healing.

Tiffani Keith is a very important person in my pack. Tiffani has supported me throughout the last several years and has listened to me about my brother, his murder, and the tremendous loss left by my brother's passing. We've spent many times just sitting in my car with the radio playing, talking about the meaning, beauty, and, yes, the tragedy of some of life's experiences. Who would know that those talks would be the foundation of our connection because she would now have the authentic, real-life experience of losing a sibling to murder, as well?

THE MOMENT LEADERS ARE BORN

Tiffani's sister Alexis (they called her Lexy; I called her beautiful) was murdered on April 25th of 2019. That day not only changed Tiffani's family forever, but forever changed the way I would view our friendship. Not that I was looking for a compadre who has lost a sibling to murder, but April 25, 2019 put Tiffani and her family on my emotional and psychological map forevermore. How could this parallel be? Does the universe really do this? Tiffani's sister, Lexy, was a very special person. She was Tiffani's sister, but she was also special to me because I can love someone in one meeting. I knew the first time that I met her that there was something really soft, kind, and graceful about her soul. She was a person who was very quick to compliment. I met her for the first time when she was with her girlfriend. The two of them seemed so opposite; her girlfriend was distant, rather cold, and seemed so different than the warmth Lexy emulated.

I remember walking away from that first meeting thinking that they were not a fit at all, that they were really not meant to be together. My intuition was right. But who knew that within the year her girlfriend, that very same girl, would shoot Lexy and take her life on April 25th, 2019 and murder her in cold blood?

I'd like to talk about that day, what I was doing that day and how it evolved, because I think it has an impact on my relationship with Tiffani, my relationship with Tiffani's family, and my relationship with Lexy's heart, soul, and being, forever.

April 25th was like many other days; my practice was working at full speed, and I was helping people become the best versions of themselves in multiple ways, really making a difference on that day. After work, I was with a friend, hanging out while he was playing cards and dominoes at a local country club.

I remember getting home around 9:00 or 9:30 p.m. and talking to

Tiffani on the phone. There are only three people in the world that have ever called me "Richard," and those include my mom (when I was in trouble), coach Tarver, and Tiffani.

"Richard, where are you?" she asked curiously.

"I'm at Cherry Hills Country Club," I said, teasing with her.

"No, you're not," she said, knowing I was pulling her leg.

"Yeah, I am," I said, kind of giggling. It was funny because she wasn't sure if I was or not, and it was kind of this little friendly sparring. We had a friendly chat during which I also confessed that she had guessed correctly and that I was already home, ready to crawl into bed after a full day. Typically, I plug my phone into the charger and set it on my nightstand, right next to my bed. For some reason that would later be quite evident, that night I left my phone on my bed next to me as I fell asleep.

As I fell asleep, I was thinking ahead to my schedule of clients, and I was anticipating what an amazing day it was going to be. I was looking forward to that as I drifted off. But when I retired to bed, little did I know that in the next six hours my life would change. At approximately 3:30 a.m., I could feel my phone vibrate on the bed. It wasn't loud, but I could feel it. I woke up, and I looked at the caller identification. It read, "BUTTERSCOTCH." "Butterscotch" is the nickname I have for Tiffani. She is bi-racial – half white, half black – hence "Butterscotch" is the endearing term I came up for her.

Gosh, she never calls me in the middle of the night, I thought. *I wonder what this is about.* Never imagining the news that was soon to follow, I answered.

"Hey girl, what's up?" I asked, half-asleep still.

"Paulette shot Lexy!" she blurted out.

"What?" I asked, not comprehending as I sat up, leaning on

one elbow and juggling the phone in my other hand, trying to understand what I thought I just heard.

She said again, "Paulette shot Lexy."

"I'm on my way," I said as I disconnected our call and jumped out of bed, grabbing my keys. I immediately threw on some clothes and ran down to my car and sped to downtown Denver to her apartment, about 12 miles away. As I approached the apartment in my car, I saw the police cars outside of her apartment. I parked and went into the lobby, where there were several police officers and detectives as well as Tiffani and another unidentified female.

I went right up to Tiffani and hugged her and held her in my arms tightly for a very long moment before I looked at her and said, "Oh baby, oh my gosh. I am here, and I love you."

She looked at me like a doe in the headlights but with great stoicism and said, "Thank you for coming so fast." Fast it was. I always wondered how fast my car would go, and that night, without incriminating myself, I found out it will go very fast.

"Where is Lexy?" I asked, looking around for any detail of what just transpired.

"The ambulance took her," she said, looking over her right shoulder.

The police officers and detectives continued to ask Tiffani questions when, after about 15 minutes, she said, "I need to go tell my mom." Her mom lived approximately 20 minutes from where we were, so naturally, I planned to drive her there. As we began to leave, one of the detectives attempted to stop us, "Well, we still have a few more questions for you." I looked at the guy and sternly said, "Look, we need to tell her mom that her daughter's just been shot. If you have any more questions for Tiffani, it can be later this morning," and we walked out.

DECISION POINT

As we drove to Tiffani's mom's house, I was thinking what that was going to be like, to walk in at approximately 4:00 am in the morning and give her that news. As we walked into Tiffani's mom's house and Tiffani told her mom what had just transpired, I could hear the screams of emotion, the panic, the elevated breathing of multiple family members as they were waking from their sleep in other rooms of the house and just learning the news. As we packed everybody into two cars, me and Tiffani in mine and the rest of the family into her mom's truck, we drove to Denver Health, which was about 20 minutes back, in the opposite direction. When we arrived at the hospital, I directed everyone to leave their cars and go ahead inside as I quickly parked the cars.

As everybody got out of the car, I gave them all hugs. "Think positive, think positive," I reassured them and hugged them tightly. First, I parked the truck, then ran back to the curb for my car. But before I could get it parked, I could feel my phone vibrating again. It was Tiffani's voice on the other end, and she quickly informed me, "Lexy didn't make it."

As I walked to the front door of the hospital, I felt the weight of the world just fall upon my shoulders, and I felt like I had been gut-punched. As I walked, I wondered where I would even find them in this big hospital, but before I even made it to the front door, they were already coming out. It all happened so rapidly. I will never forget the irony, though, as we turned around and walked towards the parking garage and saw a beautiful sunrise was occurring right before our eyes. We had just lost a beautiful, gracious, graceful human being, and before our eyes was the majesty of the most beautiful sunrise. I remember thinking to myself, *How can that be, those two contrasting pictures at that same time – moments of a beautiful sunrise and a sunset on Lexy's life?*

THE MOMENT LEADERS ARE BORN

As I reflect on it more during calmer times, I recognize and realize that beautiful sunrise was actually her spirit being lifted into the heavens, into the pearly gates. That was her. She was literally carrying that sunshine. How gorgeous, how beautiful it was for us to experience that and receive that gift of her together. I've never noticed such a beautiful sunrise in my life, and I haven't since that day; it was truly magnificent. I do believe I literally saw her soul leave that hospital and rise above us all, and I believe to this day she continues to watch over us.

So, the experience of losing my brother to murder and Tiffani losing her sister to murder are such powerful parallels in our journeys in life, and that brings a commonality to our connection. Tiffani has said to me that, when that morning happened, it became abundantly clear for her why we were put in each other's lives. I agree with that sentiment completely.

Though the murder of my brother Danny was nearly a half century ago and the loss of her sister was so fresh, I was able to give her wisdom and insight and strength for the journey that now laid before her. I look at it as bringing beauty out of Danny's death and turning it from something that attacked me to my core and hit me at my Achilles heel into strength, where I help people tremendously in need for hope and help in their own life, as it was for Tiffani.

Since the murder, my relationship with Tiffani has changed in many ways. We are still learning more and more about each other as friends. She has helped me in my business when I didn't have anybody else to help. As a true friend, I am indebted to her. But you see, Tiffani and I are bonded forever because we share the uncommon bond of losing a sibling to murder and the moments of her sister's murder and death. We will forever be connected in those ways. She is part of my pack for life.

I also have a pack of friends with whom I do life every day from a distance. We text daily and send each other encouragement. This pack is comprised of four friends, and using the first letter of each of our names forms the S.T.A.R. pack in my life.

The "S" represents Shar, who is my best female friend. The "T" represents Tiffani, who is my best friend, partner, you fill in the blank. "A" represents Amanda, an amazing, driven, eclectic human being, and the "R" is, of course, me, Richard or Rikki.

This group has provided an incredible support system for each of us, and each one of us has had a hard road to ride – Shar, for her cancer, Tiffani, for the murder of her sister, Amanda, for the breach of trust she endured, and me, for the murder of my brother. We each have been through something very traumatic in our lives. But we look to each other to support one other and help each other in many profound ways. We have a text line going with the four of us in which we send affirmations, emojis, funny sayings, and supportive words every day to let each other know that we're in each other's lives forever and there to support each other in many ways.

This is the theme of "Never hunt alone." You see, with S.T.A.R., we hunt together, we process together, we love together, and we share life's experiences together, and that's the key element that I want to emphasize – when you travel in a pack, you never have to hunt alone. If one of us is struggling, if one of us going through something, we all reach out and we build, we support and build the efficacy of that person. I am so thankful that S.T.A.R. was in full effect at my father's funeral in October 2019. During the proceedings when they performed the 21-gun salute (my dad was a World War 2 veteran) and then the bugle player played "TAPS," I literally lost my breath and gasped for air; Shar grabbed me and held on for the duration of the song as I tried to regain my breath. I will never forget that moment that my pack had my back and literally my breath.

The power of friendship in leaders is strengthened by a core community for accountability and love. And we don't just love each other, we provide accountability to each other on a consistent basis. If one of us is getting behind in our work in some way, we provide that nudge. The power in the pack is so profound because each of us has our own competencies, acumen, and skillset, and we can bring that to the pack for nurturing, growth, and wisdom.

I want to encourage you to always find a group, a powerful group, that you can attach yourself to and love, support, and hold accountable. That support group can really, really help you ride through the tough times and the trials and tribulations.

The power of friendships gives us leadership in our lives and a core community for accountability and love. Not only does this friendship group provide love, but also leadership, and we're able to express to one another what leadership looks like in our lives. I can't tell you how many times in that text line we have just sent emojis of hearts, of love, of support. Sometimes the smallest nudge is all it takes to spread love and support.

My nickname for Tiffani is "Butterscotch," or more often, "Butta," for previously mentioned reasons. My nickname for Amanda is "Money" because she was a great college basketball player that was "money" in the bank for her team. Shar is affectionately named "Wonder Woman" because one day a small child ran up to her in the mall and genuinely thought she was Wonder Woman; not to mention enduring two cancer surgeries.

We were meant to be in a pack. We were meant to be in a family. And I know this in my heart and soul because, in times when I've been alone, when I haven't had a person to love and to show love, it felt very empty.

I love to express love, feel love, be loved, give love, and I love to support and help others. Those are the core elements of a pack mentality – to be connected to each other and love and support each other as a wing man/woman, as more than that.

Through S.T.A.R., we've taught each other how to love through loss, through loss from murder, from cancer, from many violations of other people's lives. It's a powerful place to be. Leaders never hunt alone because there is power in the pack. And there's always learning, love, and growth when you're connected to others. I encourage you to go find your S.T.A.R. pack.

Tiffani's Letter to Her Sister

Alexis was someone I thought would always be here. I never considered any other way. Typing in past tense about her existence is excruciating. Thinking back to our childhood, she was always quiet. She loved doing her own hair. She had the cutest set of feet and hands a child could have. Her toes were perfectly aligned; they measured to a flawless slant. Unlike my mother's and my own feet, she had a fully placed toenail on her pinky toes. Her cheeks would puff out when she smiled, and her eyes would illuminate with happiness. She showed appreciation for the smallest acts. I loved being her big sister; it was a responsibility that I treasured. Making sure she ate, was dressed well, and was okay was all I was ever concerned with. As result of being four years older than her, we went through times of being close and distant. Lexy has always placed a high value on her friendships, so she was always at a friend's house or a friend was over at ours. She's had so many best friends; listening to all of her friends speak so highly of her was beautiful. I see pieces of Lexy in all of them. She had grace when she spoke and would listen with intent. I remember her telling me how she admired me as a big sister and a mother. I just wanted to teach her everything I knew so that she could flourish into what she was meant to be.

We went through the typical "big sister and little sister" paradigm of fighting and her taking my clothes without asking. She loved her friends so much that she would sneak my clothes for them too! But no matter where our relationship was, we were always there for each other. Lexy had always received a lot of attention when she was in middle school and high school; she innately fell into the popular crowd. Because of this, she was in the realm of drama with other girls her age. Lexy knew she had sisters who would protect her from anyone's wrath. Having two big sisters who represented different sides to any altercation, she would go to Keisha for physical protection and to me for advice on what to say or how to react. Anyone she was involved in drama with eventually mended the relationship. There were times when the girls she had previously fought would be at our home saying hi as they walked into Lexy's room; my mom, Keisha, and I would look at each other in confusion and carry on. It was her soft heart that could not hold bitterness in it. No matter what had been done, she always forgave.

Her soft heart ignited when she was around babies. Alexis had a baby when she was 15. She never complained or was scared to have her daughter, Madilynn. She embraced motherhood at such a young age. She instantly understood that she was now living for another being. She was the first to add an addition to our family; we all embraced it as a true blessing and supported her in any way we could. On my sister Keisha's 21st birthday we went out to eat as a family. Lexy had eaten too much. The family started asking her what was wrong and if she was okay, then Lexy started to cry as she covered her face. I asked her to go on a walk with me, and as we exited the restaurant she began to calm down. We sat on the curb of the sidewalk; I rubbed her back and eased out the question, "You all right?" anxious of the response I would get. To my surprise she started laughing, so I started laughing. She told me that the hormones from pregnancy made her feel overwhelmed and had her "tripping." We continued to laugh and talk about how new pregnancy is for all of us and that it's okay to cry.

Lexy had always been there for the people she loved, even if we told her not to. She held all her relationships to the same standards as family; if you needed anything, she would give it to you or help you figure out how to get it. She would take on others' problems.

Lexy is inspiring to me because of how she lived her life with the leading primacy of love. How she loved her daughter, siblings, and mom was how she loved everyone else she knew. My favorite thing about Lexy was her open heart and the love that was present whenever she engaged with anyone; it never changed.

Lexy met Paulette when she was in middle school; they dated off and on in high school and rekindled their relationship a few years ago. Paulette was living in Virginia and decided to move back to Colorado to be with Alexis. They both believed that they were each other's anchor. When we are young, it can seem acceptable to behave a certain way or to allow another to treat you in a way that is not tolerable. After discovering through my academic studies that our brains are considered fully developed at the age of 24.5, I can discern some of the decisions myself and others made as young people as immature and ignorant of the possible consequences. Growing up, we were not exposed to the best models of romantic relationships, and that could be the reason why Lexy perceived Paulette as being worthy of her love. From an observational perspective, the way the two treated each other was as if they were sisters. No, I was not fully present in their relationship and will never know of all the moments the two shared. I will never know of the many caveats that may have existed in their relationship; if Lexy had acknowledged them and taken them more seriously, she may still be here. From knowing my sister and getting to know Paulette, I could recognize that they were uncomfortable with being alone. They would break up and then next day be together again because of the fear they shared of being alone.

I have learned the significance of being alone and understand how essential it is to know oneself. It gives us the space to know ourselves and to appreciate why we are who we are. When we are alone, we can unmask ourselves of the disguises we may wear to cover our pain. It also preserves the capacity to reflect on our behavior and on that of those around us. Lexy and Paulette could hardly spend a day without the other's presence. It is important to distinguish when one is using the presence of others to fill space so that they are not alone with their self. Being comfortable with solitude is part of knowing oneself.

Weeks before I lost my sister to murder, I was in the kitchen with both her and Paulette. I observed Paulette, how she moved and how she talked in such a negative narrative. What I remember most from that day is noticing this black aura that followed Paulette. I had never seen someone's energy that surrounded their physical being, but that day it was undeniable what I saw. Days later, I was sitting in our living room with my sister. I saw it as an opportunity to talk to her about what I had seen. I asked her why she was still in this relationship with Paulette and what it was truly giving to her. My sister immediately broke down and agreed with me, but she followed up with a response that confirms her open heart and love. She said, "I know, Tiff. I know. But she doesn't have anyone. Her family is not like our family. I can't just leave her when she has nothing." Alexis told me that, once Paulette was able to sustain consistency in a job and income, she would help Paulette get on her feet, and then she would be comfortable leaving her. Looking back at this moment, I realize that what Alexis was doing was selfless. I know that if my sister understood that being with Paulette would ever jeopardize her presence in Madilynn's life, she would not have hesitated to leave that relationship.

I remember the night of April 24th and the early morning of the 25th like it was yesterday. I had put my daughter, Mia, to bed and was doing some homework. My sister's bedroom door opened, and Paulette came out. Her eyes were red, and she said it was because she had been sleeping all day. She asked me where my sister was, and I responded, "I thought she was in there with you." I called Alexis to see where she was and placed the call on speakerphone. When my sister answered, I asked her where she was, and she jokingly responded, "Girl, don't worry about it. I'll be home soon." We each said, "I love you," and hung up the phone. Paulette was drinking a slushy from Sonic. I looked at her and said, "Have a good night." But before I went to bed, I had glanced at the clock, and it happened to be 11:11 p.m. I can vividly remember wishing for my sister to make it home safely. At night I slept with my fan on to keep the temperature in my room cool. That night, I can remember questioning whether I should turn the fan on in case I needed to hear if something were to happen. I even slept with my shirt off and thought, *What if something happens and I don't have a shirt on?* I disregarded these thoughts and told myself that everything was fine; I turned the fan on and slept without a shirt.

THE MOMENT LEADERS ARE BORN

I woke up to the sound of a gunshot; I had instantly identified the sound as what I thought was my oven exploding because Paulette and Lexy were cooking something. I immediately jumped out of bed to see what was going on, opened the door to where it covered my body, squinted my eyes and yelled, "What was that sound?"

This girl, who I had mistaken for Lexy, was in my kitchen and pacing back and forth as she was screaming, "She just shot her! She just shot her!"

I responded, "Who? Who just shot who?"

She responded, "She just shot Lexy."

Before I could think I immediately started running through the house, looking for Alexis. I shouted her name, and there was no response. I looked in her room, where the light was on, and saw nothing. I ran towards the front door, where the light was coming from the hallway, and there lay my sister's body. She was gasping for air. I rushed to my knees to hold her but immediately remembered to not move someone if they are hurt because it can cause more harm. I ran to my bedroom, where Mia was asking what was wrong with Titi, her name for Lexy. I grabbed the first shirt I saw and my cell phone. I told Mia to not get off the bed and to stay right there, that Titi was fine. I dialed 911 as I ran back to my sister.

My sister was taking long, deep breaths with her eyes open. I was talking to the operator, and she asked where she was shot. I told her she was shot in the face, and the lady said to just keep talking to her. I held my sister's hand, and I told her how she had better keep breathing, that we were going to make it through this. I told her that she was going to see Madi tomorrow. I kept telling her it was going to be okay. I told her that I loved her so much. There was a point when so much blood was coming out of her mouth that I thought to go get the turkey baster so I could help remove the blood so she could breathe, but I couldn't get my legs to move. I couldn't leave my sister's side. As I held my sister's hand and looked into her eyes, I could not help but think of Paulette. I felt a deep pit of sorrow for her; to think that her mind allowed her to do such a thing to the one person in her corner was enough for me to understand that her mind was hell. I felt pity for her that her actions had driven her to this point. It's challenging to put into words, but in that moment, I felt Lexy forgive her for this. My heart knew Lexy was not going to make it, but my mind could not face it.

My relationship with Paulette was different from my family's relationship with her because I welcomed her into my home, and I loved her because my sister loved her. I recall going to retail stores to buy her an outfit so that she could look presentable in interviews. I learned that the origin of her pain was from her older sister dying; it was deemed suicide, but Paulette believed that the guy her sister had been living with had murdered her. Her family had a great amount of distance between them – so much that Paulette would question the closeness of our family. Paulette did not know love like we did. She had never really processed her pain. I can remember how she often would finish sentences with, "Yea, but everything is everything." I wanted to lead her to a deeper understanding of herself, so I challenged her to explain to me what that saying meant to her. She could not conceptualize what it meant to her, so I asked her to just sit down one day and write what that meant to her. That never happened, but that night that was all just a distant memory.

As I sat there waiting for the ambulance, I rocked myself back and forth as I held my sister's hand; I repeated the words, "This is my pain." For the previous year or so, I had a persistent thought that would flow through my head every now and then, especially at family dinners. The thought was about soaking up the moments of that day with my family and being grateful for the sense that everything was okay. In this moment, everything was not okay; there was pain and I tried to absorb it and hold it for her. There are a lot of us in my family; eleven of us would meet at my mom's place every Sunday to participate in family dinner. We considered Sunday the day that we all got to reunite and touch base to make sure everyone was okay. Sunday dinners were meant to maintain some form of control of the distance that being an adult can create by having our own lives and living separately. The feeling of being okay is simply underrated. I desperately wanted everything to be okay as I sat next to my sister laying on the floor next to me.

As the police and paramedics got there, I stepped away to comfort Mia. It was only Mia and I that knew what had just occurred and that Lexy might be gone for forever. I could not think to deliver this news to my mother, so I decided to call the one person I knew I could depend on in such a horrendous time: Richard.

I had known Richard for five years at this point. Our relationship was founded on sharing the stories from our childhoods and adulthoods that contributed to our present selves. Hearing Richard's story of losing Danny at the age of seven had illuminated the beauty in pain that he had experienced. I had never met someone who had experienced such a tragedy yet flourished from it. He decided what the pain would do for him; he conquered his pain in the most incredible way by living and sharing it every day. Looking back at it, Richard is the template my mind has formed on how one lives with such tragedy.

As I pulled away from my sister and allowed the paramedics to step in, I knew Lexy was gone, but I could not bear to tell my mom that or hear the doctor tell me alone that she had not made it. As we drove to my mother's house, where my mom and siblings slept,

DECISION POINT

I thought about how this would be the last night that they would be able to sleep with a full heart.

It's strange how objects can bookmark a moment. That morning when I returned to my apartment to get clothes to take to my mom's, I glanced at the Sonic cup Paulette had been drinking out of just twelve hours before, when my sister was still alive. When I left my apartment, my sister, Keisha, and I drove to the coroner to pick up my sister's belongings. As we drove, Keisha had been playing music from her phone on the stereo. Unexpectedly and on it's own, the stereo switched from Bluetooth to radio and began to switch through different stations and stopped at a station where Lexy's favorite song was playing – "Always Be My Baby" by Mariah Carey. Keisha and I immediately begin to cry; my tears were partial joy because I interpreted this strange occurrence as my little sister telling me that she was okay, that she made it to the other side.

When I had to share with the detectives how the events unfolded moments before Lexy was shot, I can recall describing Alexis and Paulette's relationship as two broken people just trying to find something whole. The moment those words left my mouth, I immediately knew that it was not what I intended to say. As the journey in court began, my family shared how Paulette's defense had used my statement to favor Paulette. This broke my heart because I felt as though I had misrepresented my sister. Alexis was not a broken person at all. And I should have never categorized her in the same group as Paulette. According to societal constructs, she may have been lacking in having a consistent job or living independently. Those achievements do not define who you are. What defines you is how you treat others. My sister was not broken, because Alexis was love; she knew to give love, how to be selfless, how to value others. She put others ahead of herself. There will be people who have obtained the success that society deems acceptable but who will die without knowing what it means to love or be loved. Alexis knew love. What is not love is a call for love; Alexis was love and, she wanted to bring Paulette to know love.

When Lexy left, a piece of me left. Somehow, I instinctively knew that I could not grieve in the ways I had observed others grieve; it just did not suit me. Lexy being gone is something my mind and heart still struggle to grasp; one day my heart may fathom it, but my brain is completely discombobulated by the thought that I will never see my sister again. In the moments where the pain appears insurmountable, I yell to the clouds, "I love you, Lex." Since she left, I have felt a significant shift in my predominant lens for life. It's as if I've begun to pull off the shallow parts of my life like bark on a tree. I could tell you 100 times that life is fleeting, but until you consciously experience a moment where life fled you, you may never fully understand. Losing someone I anticipated to love for forever to murder has caused my benchmark for pain to heighten extensively. So has my appreciation in life and capacity to love. I understand that there are not many things that can occur today that will bring the same emotions I experienced from the loss off my sister.

Somehow, losing Alexis has given me the permission to be myself, and maybe that is because Alexis does not get the opportunity to. I know that my sister and I truly enjoyed each other, and I can hear her tell me to be me, to ask that question I am thinking, and to bring energy to all things I encounter without hesitation. We would laugh so much when we were together, she gave me permission to be silly and I don't find myself being silly with many others. We would laugh so much that I would question if she really thought I was funny and that would make us laugh even more.

Her life was cut way too short. I get to speak for my sister in this dimension, and having that responsibility has assembled me with passion, compassion, and empathy that could only be orchestrated through such tragedy. My life was not as fruitful before I knew this power of pain. Surprisingly, I had more bad days before I lost my sister than I do today. There is just too much to appreciate in this world that I hope to never take for granted. In the past I would allow nuisances to overtake my days, such as getting a flat tire unexpectedly or receiving poor service from a restaurant. It is funny because now, I find myself saying the same things as Richard would, like, "I'm just thankful to be eating." My life has experienced an immense amount of darkness because of the loss of my sister, from waking up to my mother crying to walking Madilynn through ways she can cope with missing her mother. Because of this great amount of darkness, the small things that bring light, such as getting to experience my family another Sunday, truly make a difference.

As I attended my sister's funeral, I listened to the many friends who shared their experiences with Alexis. In every friend, I saw my sister. I saw a young girl who covertly sought guidance. They were all beautiful young ladies who had love in their hearts but had been leading themselves based on what they had only observed others doing, such as tolerating domestic violence or comporting themselves into identities that did not match their hearts. It limits our abilities, unknowingly, when we adopt behaviors from others without introspecting why. I know that my steady positive outlook has buffered me for some of the pain of losing my sister. There is nothing that I can do to bring my sister back physically, and I have fully accepted this. By accepting it, I have decided to relieve any thought concerning a hypothetical "what if" because all that can do is instill regret from an only imagined reality that is not serving me. What brings me peace when I think of Lexy is that I know she knew how much I loved her. I can recall passing each other in the hallways of our home and randomly saying to each other, "I love you, Girl." Or we would be cooking, and I would stop to tell her that I am proud of her and her achievements. I often shared with her what I was thinking of her because I knew it would build her up to be who she was supposed to be.

It is important to understand that Lexy is not gone; she is still very much present on my team, just in a different way now. I can remember how much I loved guiding Lexy to greater awareness, and my heart still yearns to do that. Since my sister passed, I've begun a group called Lexy's Girls, where Lexy's friends and other women can come together and talk about stuff that is significant to our hearts. I was given the ability to cultivate a space where women can talk about the things that weigh on their hearts and receive a variety of perspectives; this is my therapy. Gathering with these girls has made my pain penetrable because I still get to experience my sister through them.

Where my family comes from, we are modeled living from a survival point. We were never taught of the importance behind identity and your own perception of self. Today, I understand that our self-concept is our leading impetus for where we are in our lives. It influences how we treat ourselves and value others. The way we interpret the world is painted by our self-concept because we can perceive life happening to us or that we are in control of it. When you are able to conceptualize who you are verbally, not only does the brain hear it, but also you begin to believe it. Alignment is established when communion in ourselves is found; only then can we begin to create authentic communion with others. I strive to instill the importance of a self-concept in the Lexy's Girls group because I believe that if Lexy would have established a self-concept of who she was and who she was not, it would have elucidated her perceived compatibility in her romantic relationship as illusion. Solid self-concepts should be impervious to external occurrences; what happens outside of you does not dictate your values and your comportment.

I am the only person in my family to complete a college degree. I have found that my college career is the foundation of my self-efficacy for a multitude of reasons. Attending college and being from a family where no one came close to finishing sheds adversity where I had to teach myself what perseverance was with no one there to model it. Having a daughter at 21, I was in the middle of completing my 4-year Bachelor's degree program. I decided to adopt the lens of being an outlier and trudging through by raising my daughter, independently, and continuing school. I noticed how college supported my ability to think independently and to seek an antithesis.

Losing Alexis has been my greatest lesson; I invite the pain in so that I can learn all that I am able to. I want to learn as much as I can from the loss of my sister so that I can teach others the beauty in this life. You will find out who you truly are in the storm; and whatever you want to change, you can. You just have to make the decision to. My pain summoned my power; this is my pain, Alexis, you are my fuel. The picture below 9-1, illuminates the grace and beauty in Lexy's soul. Richard described her as magnetic and pure ataraxia.

Over here is all for you, Lex.

This is the last photo captured with us four on April 6th, 2019, 19 days before Alexis passed. To have the opportunity to raise Madi and Mia as sist-ousins (sisters and cousins) is a role that brings me the most joy. I get to see Alexis in Madilynn every day. From left to right: Alexis, Mia, my mom, Kim, Madilynn and me, Tiffani.

Chapter Ten

THE PSYCHOLOGY OF LEADERSHIP

What is leadership and what does true leadership look like? The answers that come to mind will be somewhat different for many people but have some similarities; we all expect leaders to lead, to make something out of nothing, to inspire others to actions and results, and to be good role models. When leaders can influence other people and inspire great results, we definitely put them in the leadership category.

Can you name a few leaders who come to mind? You might think of Winston Churchill, Dr. Martin Luther King Jr., John F. Kennedy, Peyton Manning, Rosa Parks, Rodolfo "Corky" Gonzales. Why do we think of them as leaders? Is it their achievements, success, or ability to make tough decisions under pressure, perhaps? Maybe it was their great wisdom, courage, integrity, accountability, and determination to stay in the fight that leads to great victories. Yes, we can probably all agree, because of the character traits they demonstrated, they were all great leaders. But what determines someone as a good leader, and are leaders born or made?

A good leader is typically defined by their record of successes and victory, but also by our personal perceptions and principles of what great leadership looks like. I would say both – a leader is born,

144

but also made – because who a person is at their core, impacts the way they will show up in the world to serve others and make decisions for the greater good. A leader is also made because a leader is forged through the fires of life. I have shared several meaningful stories of people I have encountered and the leadership qualities they demonstrated. Many reveal these traits because of the traumas and tragedies they have faced and their moments of decision when they decided the path they would take to show up in the world in spite and because of these experiences.

What is leadership? If you don't already have a definition, you may quickly discount the leader in you. Do you see yourself as a leader? When I give presentations, often, I begin the presentation by asking the show of hands, "How many people in this room are leaders?" Usually, I get about a third of the audience that will raise their hands. But by the end of my presentation, I ask that same question, and everyone raises their hand. Why the change of vision or heart? Weren't they the same participants from the beginning of my speak? Yes, but they had changed their perspective and now were able to see themselves as leaders.

First, I want to begin with leadership. The topic is broad, and we will cover many areas, including "The Big Five," a concept I call leadership/followership, top principles I use as a guide to personal leadership, the importance of gender and culture in leadership, qualities of a leader, listening, always anticipating what's just around the corner by staying one step ahead, how leaders honor the past, how games are won off the field, how loss is the golden opportunity of life, and winning at life through the choices we make.

DECISION POINT

The Big Five:

- Transformational
- Transactional
- Autocratic
- Charismatic
- Reverent

The Big Five are the primary five leadership styles we use in organizations today. *The Bass Handbook of Leadership* (2008) is a very good reference and explains the various leadership/followership styles in greater detail. Before we begin diving into the core elements of leadership, please let me clarify an aspect of leadership that is not delineated enough: The difference between climate and culture: Often, we hear that a coach or a CEO wants to lead the change of the culture of an organization; well, they better change the climate first, because the climate is the mood, the communique and behavior that is occurring right now in an organization. So, the way to begin to change the culture of a team or organization, is to have a strategic plan that addresses the climate *and* the culture of the organization. Climate is now, culture is established and cultivated over time.

Transformational leadership literally transforms organizations in climate and culture; that is, it changes communication and behavioral tendencies. Examples of people with this leadership style are CEOs, head coaches, and political leaders. Transformational leaders motivate their followers to do more than the followers originally intended and thought possible. Transactional leaders oversee the transactions of medium to small groups. This type of leader is typically middle to upper management. They tend to be very hands-on, good communicators, and great with people. Autocratic leaders are very structured and disciplined; this type of leader is prominent in the military, law enforcement, and corrections. Charismatic leaders have charisma; they lead by being excellent communicators and people oriented. However, what these leaders achieve, that is rare, is human connection. They evoke emotion from their followers, which impacts their thoughts, feelings, mood, and behavior. They can be CEO types but more often are independent leaders, like entrepreneurs, entertainers, and creators; they move people with not only their words, but also with their nonverbal communication, gestures, and expressions. Further, Reverent leaders are probably the most underrated leaders of all. They are simply workers who do their jobs every day in a proficient way. This behavior is illuminated in front of other workers, and they become models for others to emulate. As such, they are very powerful in changing communication and behavior in the organizational context. Like a pebble in a pond, their behavior literally ripples through the organization that shows itself as Reverent leadership. It's quiet, its covert, but it's so powerful that it literally works from the inside out. Twenty years ago, we did not even identify this behavior as leadership, but merely as a good worker; we now conceptualize it differently. As such, isn't everyone in your organization a leader? A leader of their own behavior? Organizations have traditionally viewed leaders as verbal, vocal and visual, the typical Transformational or Charismatic leader; however, we now know that leaders deliver their messages in divergent ways that reach people at all levels of the organization. Therefore, everyone is a leader in some context.

My goal with exploring leadership is that you begin to see yourself as a leader; everyone is a leader and has the capacity to lead. Leadership begins by simply being the best version of yourself and modeling for the rest of your team what excellence looks like. That is truly a form of Reverent leadership. Reverent leadership refers to an environment of collaboration and influence, rather than command and control. When you show up and do your best, your colleagues, coworkers, and teammates notice the work you're doing; your leadership becomes influential and creates a climate and culture of collaboration. You are basically modeling for the rest of your team how to do things the right way. This is a strong form of leadership, modeling for others to emulate and follow.

Really, everyone generally fits into one, or perhaps a few of the big five leadership styles. How do you see your leadership style now that I have briefly illuminated their tendencies?

Leaders are born to lead, which essentially means we were each born to lead – someone or something – and as we develop our character traits, our values, our defining principles, and then experience and emerge from the trials and fires of life, our inner leader is then revealed, and our leadership style is molded and developed. I do want to emphasize that, as important as leadership is, we must also value followership, which is necessary, by definition, for leaders to be leaders. They must, in theory, have followers. There's not enough emphasis put on followership in our culture. As I said, if you don't have followers, leadership doesn't exist. Who are you leading? You must have followers to have leadership, and it is inherent of leadership that one leads by inspiring others to follow. With that comes great responsibility; it is not for ego-driven purposes, which some leaders can get caught up in.

The psychology of understanding followership is paramount to good leadership – leaders must understand their followers to lead with integrity and success. Who are your followers? What are their listening styles? What are their communication styles? What are their goals and objectives in following you? Leaders and followers can sometimes trade roles; it's called power sharing. There is a straightforward yet divergent interdependence between leadership and followership. If you were to search, you would find hundreds of leadership conferences but very few, if any, conferences on followership. And yet, understanding followership is paramount to strong leadership.

I suggest leaders spend more time understanding their followers; their psychology, if you will. Here is an important principle to remember: Get to know your followers. Who are your followers, their demographics, their age, their education level, their ethnicity, their cultural practices and norms? What motivates them? What are their emotions? When we talk about emotional intelligence, for example, how emotionally intelligent is your audience? How mindful is your audience? These are practices that we teach and can tell us much about the disposition and emotional stability of a follower. Are there people in your audience that are willing to leave their comfort zone? This will help you understand who will follow and how they will follow and should offer good clues in developing a leadership strategy.

It is vital for us as leaders to understand who our followers are, what they are made of, how they think, and how they are motivated. There's a real followership–leadership interdependence. Another element to understand the psychology of followership is that followers must consent to being led. Their consent to your leadership will determine if they are willing to "drink your Kool-Aid." They need to believe in what you do and what you stand for and share your vision for the mission and the direction you are asking them to move in.

Followership isn't only about accepting your content; it's the delivery of that content that is very important. Do they look up to you as a leader? Have they determined they want to emulate you or your practices and are hence willing to follow you? Have they consented to your authority and your vision? Do they want access to you, and are they willing to lay down their own direction to take up your cause and follow you to victory?

The next step is followership empowerment. Leaders empower followers for optimal success and in service to others, to encourage their personal growth. Leadership 20 or 30 years ago meant that leaders led, and followers followed. But now one of the greatest ways to empower followership in an organization is to allow them to also lead themselves, allow them to lead their own team, allow them to lead their own behavior, allow them to set goals for their own personal development. When working with professional athletic teams in the NFL, MLB and NBA, I encourage head coaches to allow the players lead a practice and design the periods that make-up a practice content. This level of empowerment of followers is vital for their leadership development. It also creates a warm environment for the connection and respect it creates towards the leader. It is vital to understand the psychology between leadership and followership for optimal outcomes.

It is true, leadership and followership are impacted by the climate and culture of the team or organization. Is there an environmental fit for this leadership style? Is there a fit for the followership? Do they enjoy the work that they're doing and want to personally grow or follow for a larger vision? For example, in industrial-organizational psychology (I/O), we define three levels of occupation: job, career, and calling. Ideally, all followers would be in a position they considered their "calling," but that's not always the case. Sometimes a person is in a position because they followed a career path but never actually desired such a position. Sometimes it's simply a job to them. These ideas may play a factor in followership.

Followers have just as much power, or perhaps more, as leaders because if they do not consent, then their leadership is falling on deaf ears. Followers must be willing to follow, willing to be led. Sometimes, their emotions and motivation are impacted based on the weight of their position as it is defined to them by calling, career, or job.

The final point of the interdependence between leadership and followership is power sharing when planning change. When you're going to implement change, one of the most collaborative things leaders can do is involve the followership and share the power. When you share your power with followers, it empowers them. It creates a wider circle of trust, and cooperation follows. Everyone wants to feel as if they have a purpose and play a significant role in the outcome of success. Leaders don't hold on to the reigns or the power too tightly; they serve others, honor others, and include others. In turn, the team is strengthened and diversified, and the goals are reached.

Now, let's talk more about the qualities of a leader. I've often said that leaders in the old style were verbal, vocal, and visual. Followers received communiqué, usually directives, often postulating an autocratic style of communication and behavior. However, the qualities of a leader have changed over time. Leaders aren't as verbal or vocal or as authoritarian as they once were; styles have relaxed, cultures have changed, and followers are now included at the table of most companies and teams.

How leaders look has also changed. They are not always the oldest one on the team, not always the most educated or best dressed. Now, it is not unusual for younger professionals who are dressed casually to speak in sentence fragments and ride skateboards to work leading a divergent group of followers. When I was in California for Super Bowl 50 with the Broncos, I gave a presentation on the Apple campus in Cupertino, California and was both surprised and happy that one of their leaders literally rides a skateboard 10 blocks to work.

DECISION POINT

"Teamwork makes the dream work," and in this style of leadership climate and culture, there is usually a place for everyone's contribution. The one thing that all leaders do still have is creativity, drive, vision, desire, initiative, and a motive. A motive, which is the root word of motivation, is the number one quality that is important in a leader – a motive for deploying leadership. This is not age-associated, but a differentiator.

Where does the motive come from? It can be environmentally based or genetically based. For leaders to be great, not good, they need to delineate and embrace their motive. One of the first things we do when we train leaders is help them understand how important our communication skills are. Communication skills training is vital because you can have all the great knowledge in the world, but if you do not communicate in an effective way that is digestible for the follower, then oftentimes your leadership will fall on deaf ears. It's important that we emphasize this because, again, you can have knowledge, awareness, and insight, but it must be communicated in a way that can be effectively ingested and digested by your followers.

If you're a leader in an organization, communication skills are key to success. It creates an opportunity to be understood or to be misunderstood, and it puts the team at risk for failure if it isn't clear. All of your communication as a leader is not always going to be written; much of it will be spoken. As it's spoken, a leader needs to be discerning and intentional with the ability to speak clearly, enunciate, understand different vernaculars of the team, and correspond to the audience. Sensitivity to those you are speaking to, the culture of the organization, and the environment in which you are communicating are all equally important. The nonverbal aspect of communication – posture, gestures, voice inflection, even the clothes you are wearing – are vital in terms of communication skills training. So, it's imperative that we understand a great quality of a leader is their communication skills – verbal and nonverbal. If you're willing to work on your communication skills, you can be a great communicator. Leaders step up their game when facing others, and they sharpen their communication skills in order to relate to all.

I once heard national champion football coach Lou Holtz speak at a business symposium, and I thought it was very interesting that he didn't say anything about football, but rather focused on being a better communicator. He talked about leadership and business acumen.

"Be a great communicator. Not a good one, but a great communicator," he said. And I've never forgotten that. That's an important and vital aspect to a quality as a leader.

At the risk of overindulgence, I really want to emphasize the importance of communication skills. One of my master's degrees is in human communication and rhetoric. To me, there is an under emphasis on oral communication skills in our primary training pipelines like our formal educational systems. For example, I once taught public speaking at the university level; often, students would come into that class with a deficit base regarding public speaking. In other words, they often dreaded the notion of speaking in public. I have always found this interesting because I absolutely love speaking in public. There is a whole psychology to public speaking and it's that speakers often feel that they will be judged or analyzed; as such, they tend to be apprehensive at getting up in front of people where judgement could occur. Because of this dynamic, many speakers never reach their true potential because they frame the process as mere survival as opposed to an opportunity at developing a skillset that can truly impact their life in profound ways. I can honestly say that speaking in front of teams, organizations and audiences in general, is one of my favorite parts of being a performance psychologist.

One of the most important things about communication skills is listening. In the United States we talk about how important listening is to communication. But I don't think we walk the walk. If you look at our educational system in the universities across America, the majority of these institutions teach public speaking skills and orator skills, which is focused on communication that is verbal and vocal. But very few of them teach a semester-long course on listening, which is the messages we receive. I think that's really important to understand because if you're not a great listener, it's hard to be an exceptionally effective communicator or leader. It's similar to the dynamics between leadership and followership. Where, theoretically you need followers to have leaders, especially effective leaders, in order to be a communicator or a speaker, a giver of information, you must have listeners, receivers of communication.

In America, we're a very power-oriented country; that's one of the reasons why we emphasize speaking more and not listening as much. In most communication skills books or interpersonal communication textbooks, one of the last chapters will have to do with either cultural aspects of communication or the listening piece. They will tack on a chapter on listening but not put a real emphasis on it.

Listening skills are vital to our ability to communicate effectively because if we do not listen, we do not understand what the sender of the message is attempting to communicate. It is essential to understand the sender–receiver model in communication. Here is a basic rendition of the sender/receiver model often depicted in human communication and rhetoric. Although rudimentary in its framework, its implications and contextualism is profound for leaders. While most leaders fine tune their KSA's (knowledge, skills, abilities) related to the delivery of messages, both written and spoken, its somewhat uncommon to find leaders that consistently work specifically on their listening skills. The illustration below depicts how important it is to understand the sender/receiver concept and that human communication is a two-way street with several variables and factors influencing the transmission of effective communication between two people.

Sender-Receiver Human Communication Model

Factors that influence communication:

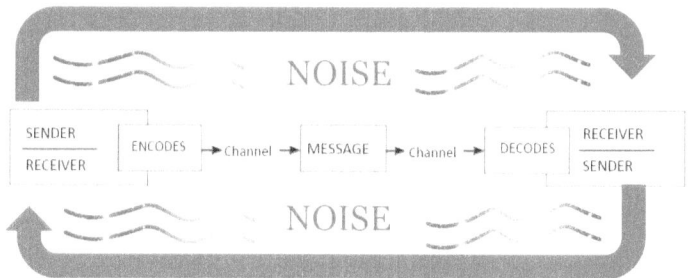

We are sending and receiving messages simultaneously.

Where Communication Breaks Down
Sources of Noise/Interference:

- Communication/Listening styles
- Cultural differences
- Gender/Sex
- Generational
- Regionalism
- Differences in language/vocabulary/vernacular
- Defensiveness/Sympathetic Nervous System

DECISION POINT

A fundamental aspect of the sender–receiver model is, firstly, the leader's involvement in the communication exchange. How are they delineating their thoughts, intentions and delivering that message in a purposeful and concise communication that is received as it was intended from the sender, in this case, the leader.? It is critical for leaders to be great communicators. The sender–receiver model gives us a clear illustration of how this works. The sender of a particular message has to consider who the receiver of the message is and also consider all aspects impacting and influencing the receiver. Great leaders are sensitive in their leadership to all genders, cultures, and races. You don't want to send a message that's egocentric or ethnocentric. The sender's communication skills, and thus their thinking skills, should pay attention to the wants and needs of the receivers; the whole person should be taken into account and especially their personality. Multiple factors are to be considered before any word is spoken or delivered. A leader must consider demographics, age, education level, ethnicity, and cultural practices and norms. Without this careful sensitivity, there's too much noise in that channel from sender to receiver that could distort the message. Finally, let's not forget that the receivers of a particular message are simultaneously senders of nonverbal messages as well. In fact, when nonverbal communication is taken into consideration, senders are receivers and receivers are senders. Body language is a strong and reliable form of communication. In fact, in the scholarly world of human communication, we deem that nonverbal communication is more reliable than verbal communication, being that a particular person can lie about their intentions verbally. One's body language rarely takes us astray from core behavior. Eye-contact, posture, gestures, and breathing all tell us a great deal about a person's intent and purpose

Communication is the number one area or construct that impacts most intimate relationships, as well. Relationships don't go well when the sender of a message does not consider what the receiver of the message is thinking or how they're attaching meaning and value to it in receiving a particular message. As mentioned previously, we must remember that, while a sender is sending messages, a receiver is receiving but also sending messages nonverbally. It's a complex and fluid relationship between sender and receiver. Perhaps this is why sometimes communications are "clear as mud," but this can rarely be the case for leaders if success is to be achieved. Leaders who are also great communicators take into account the sender–receiver model and are accountable for sending a message that is consistent with the behavioral, and communication practices of the receiver of the message. This practice will enhance the opportunity for successful communication and conveying the true intent of a message so that it can also be received in the same way as it was intended to be received.

Great communicators are also great listeners, and that's a major aspect of receiving messages. There must be a reciprocal relationship between leaders and followers, but there also must be a reciprocal relationship between senders and receivers of messages. In effective leadership, listening is as key as communicating. As leaders, we must listen while we lead. We typically only emphasize the speaking part when we lead. I've coined the term "The Three V's of Leadership," which encompasses verbal, visual, and vocal aspects of communicating, but the true key to effective communication is listening; adhering to what people around you are postulating in terms of their thoughts, needs, and wants. Some of the greatest leaders in the world are some of the best listeners; but too often in our culture, we're considered quiet, reserved, even passive when we take the time to listen. Leaders often fill the space by talking to get their point across. Being passive and quiet to listen is often seen as weak leadership, but, talking just to talk is not effective communication and not a sign of strength for leaders. The listening aspect is vital to great leadership, so we must listen while we lead to be most effective.

When we listen, it gives us the advantage of being one step ahead. Great leaders are always anticipating what might come around the corner, thus listening with intent. While we want to emphasize mindfulness, which really is about being present in the moment, we also must be listening for flags and indicators that allow us to respond one step ahead of any crisis or necessary response.

As Will Rogers said, "Don't let yesterday use up too much of today." Simply be present. While that is true to regulate the autonomic nervous system – to keep anxiety and fear and the residual adrenaline rush at bay and also keep you in that parasympathetic side of your nervous system – it's always important to also be one step ahead in your thinking and receiving of information and to anticipate what the future might require of you as a leader to navigate you and your team to success, so that you can guide and lead your team effectively. "One step ahead" is simply about reflecting as you listen, putting the information through an action filter, so to speak, and anticipating what you're going to do or how you are going to respond so you can be ready for appropriate action.

As leaders, we sometimes distribute what I call "sugar and vinegar communication." Sugar communique are messages that are sweet and complimentary in base. Conversely, vinegar communique is mostly tart, hard-to-swallow, often corrective feedback. Addressing all aspects of communication, including nonverbal and vocal messages, and then responding without charge, such as using "I" messages, can help to deliver vinegar communication with strength and yet, help the receiver step outside of personalizing the message, thus receiving it in a positive light rather than negatively or personally.

Great communicators restructure their language to a certain extent and intentionally, seamlessly, work on avoiding the use of absolute language or emotionally charged words. Here's an example of a communication style that gets people into a trap: In a marital relationship, for example, a wife may say to a husband, "You always forget to take out the trash," in her frustration of one final situation. She doesn't really mean *always*; she means occasionally. So, if we can remember to say what we mean with care to our every word and mean what we say by carefully expressing ourselves through our language, our word construction and selection, and also our nonverbal inflections and body language, we can avoid most mis-communication and become more effective in our messages for healthier relationships and positive outcomes.

In our life and executive coaching programs in our practice, we have what's called the red, yellow, and green boxes of word selection. The red box contains words like, "Wow, this is going to be hard; it's going to be tough. I don't know if I can do this." That's not the box we want to live in. The yellow box is really a question box like, "I'll give it a try. I'll try to get it done. Maybe." We really want to eliminate the words *try* and *problem* from our vocabulary. We don't try things; we do things. We may not accom-plish them in the timeframe we want to, but we are going to do things as opposed to try things. And *problem* is a stop word. We don't want that word in our vocabulary. What we do want in our vocabulary is *challenge*. Replace the word *problem* with *challenge* because it's going to be a challenge, but we're going to do it. So that's a key aspect of language reconstruction. The green box is where we want to live, with words and phrases like, "I will get it done. I will accomplish my objectives and goals. It's done." These words and phrases are affirmative, clear, and positive.

We call the "always," "you never," "you always," absolute language. That's really not effective communication because it is not a true indicator of reality. Leaders are careful to "say what you mean and mean what you say." If it's occasionally, say that. If it's often, say that. If it's once in a while, say that. But don't say "always" when you mean "occasionally." I cannot emphasize enough how important word selection is for effective communicators, orators, and consequently leaders.

Great leaders are careful and intentional with their words. They understand there are many aspects and dynamics of communication. Leaders are on top of their communication game with active listening and appropriate response. Leaders are sensitive to whom they are communicating. Leaders are humble in their communication and they learn from history. Leaders learn from their mistakes, challenges, trials, and tribulations. All are a breeding ground for growth and development.

In my practice I often tell my clients, "There's beauty in the struggle." Struggle is actually an opportunity for growth and development and not to be seen as only a struggle or a tribulation. Leaders learn and experience growth that is vital to rising as a leader. When leaders frame negative situations as opportunities as opposed to great tragedies, we are reframing situations as periods to learn, grow, and become better versions of ourselves, stronger and more effective leaders, true contributors to society, and strength for those around us. Through our growth, we can turn to others and become helpers and transform other people's lives. Struggles are real, crises in life are often inevitable, but like the butterfly, the leader only emerges from the cocoon after the struggle to freedom from the fear or the crisis in front of them. From adversity comes growth, and true leaders are born. Fire forges the iron.

Great leaders and communicators honor the past and move forward. It's not that leaders aren't human or don't experience emotions in times of crisis; it is more about how they address the crisis emotionally, how they process through it and emerge from it, that reveals their true character and develops them as leaders of the pack.

For all of us, there are things that happened in our past that challenge us and change us, and I'll use my father's recent death as an example. My dad passed away in late September 2019. To me, he was a titan of a man. He lived to be 99 years old, and my family and I were already planning his 100th birthday party. Initially, it was very challenging knowing my father was not around anymore. I couldn't stop by his house and say hello. I couldn't pick up the phone and say, "Hey, can I bring the boys over?" But now I can hold him up and lift him up in spirit and represent him in my business, in my practices, in my relationships, the kind of quality person and quality man that he was.

It's important how, as a leader, I frame this very deep and painful event. It as an opportunity for personal growth as opposed to a loss. Leaders honor the past, learn from the past, respect the past and the lessons it showed them but then move on and move forward. Your victory is in the lessons learned. This is very much like the concept that games are won off the field. A lot of people will say, "Hey, it's game day," and it's important what you bring out there on game day. But in the NFL, for example, most teams play on Sunday, sometimes Monday night, sometimes Thursday night, and then later in the season on Saturdays. But the games on Sunday are usually won on Wednesday, Thursday, and Friday, and even on Mondays in the meeting rooms after the games while reviewing the tape.

DECISION POINT

Preparation is really where we win the games and come to victory and go on to win the Super Bowl.

Preparation is paramount. It's really the thing that prepares us for when we go to battle for victory. While we always put a big emphasis on the day we are giving a presentation, on the day we're playing a game, on the day that we have a test, it's vitally important to remember how important those days of preparation are. We call it "putting the hay in the barn." I mean, have you done your work to move you towards the victory? Have you done what it takes to execute when you get out on the field?

Traditionally, Tuesday is a day off for NFL teams but not for coaches. Coaches win with their game planning on Tuesday. If they don't put together a good game plan for the upcoming Sunday, then they are in a deficit even before they teach and coach the players for the game. Just as preparation is a golden key to winning, loss is the golden opportunity of life. I've often said that when you lose a game you really reflect, dive deep and assess what worked, what didn't and why the outcome wasn't different. You look in the mirror and say, "What could we have done differently?" When you win a game, oftentimes you celebrate it for a bit and then you move on. It's the loss that really makes you stop and examine your life, your team, and all the elements and variables involved.

Loss of life, my father passing away, some of the deaths and murders that have been chronicled in this book, have really made me take a look at my life. Going back to when I was seven years old, I'm convinced, 100% convinced, that if I had not experienced that loss, I would not be the person I am today. I would not have the energy, the passion, the drive, the fierce determination, or the mindset that I've got to live every day to its fullest.

At seven years old I learned that things can be over in an instant, and I've been very, very cognizant of living my life in a very present mode and model to honor my brother. Oftentimes I say I'm living a life for two; that's why I have so much energy, so much passion, so much strength and drive to get to a point of excellence. So, loss is the golden opportunity of life, an opportunity for personal growth and to live your future life differently. Loss is the breeding ground for growth and development.

Finally, I'm going to talk about winning at life through the choices we make. Everything in life is a choice. I will repeat that: Everything in life is a choice. How do we choose to comport ourselves every day? Our communication style, our behavior, our clothing, our jewelry, choosing life's relationships – everything is a choice. I was recently speaking to a college basketball team, and up on the wall they had the list of All Americans, the list of players-of-the-year, etc.

"Look up at those walls," I directed. "You probably think those players were chosen to be All Americans by their peers or by the press and the media, and they essentially were." But I also said, "They chose an All-American lifestyle. They chose a player-of-the-year lifestyle. They pushed, they stretched, they were disciplined and structured."

It's vital to understand that how you choose to live your life will influence every aspect of your life. Becoming an All American, becoming an All Pro, becoming a CEO of a company, becoming excellent as a mother, as a father, as a husband, as a wife, as a partner – those are choices we make. Everything in life is a choice. If we don't understand that and we think that life really falls upon us, then we're missing a big opportunity to become what we choose to become. Don't get me wrong, life does often fall upon us – like with unexpected tragedies – but we also have choices every day in how we respond to those challenges. In our practice, we have what is called the 10/90 rule as mentioned earlier: This asserts that life is 10% of what happens in life and 90% of how we respond to that occurrence. When Michael Jordon was cut from his varsity basketball team, he did not give up; in fact, he used that situation to respond with an unimaginable effort that would one day make him one of the greatest players to ever walk this planet. As such, the choices we make are vital to winning in life. When you choose excellence, you choose a lifestyle. When you choose mediocrity, you choose a lifestyle. And from both of those choices, you will get the results you are looking for. Every choice you make has an impact on your life and your leadership and your future.

Whatever we decide to do, we make choices along the way. When we talk about a decision point, there's a point where you make a decision in life, where you choose greatness, where you choose the ability to really be where you want to be in life. Something's different, you have made a clear vision, a higher choice, and have determined to go after it; it has become part of the fabric of who you are, but it starts in that moment in time, the moment of decision, that decision point when you make a choice. You choose how to show up and who you are. Everything is a choice.

Demarcus Ware: Leaders Decide to Make a Decision

Everyone has to wake up and make a choice, a decision, how they are going to accept their fears and shortcomings. Everyone reaches their breaking point where they have to make a decision. When I left the Dallas Cowboys and came to the Denver Broncos, I was a little lost as a person. I had everything in the world materialistically – cars, houses, anything you could put in a cardboard box. Or so I thought, until I saw you, Dr. P. You taught me how to be real, authentic, and true to myself.

THE MOMENT LEADERS ARE BORN

You have so many devices and machines at your office, but it was our one-on-one talks that set me free. I am indebted to you forever for helping me discover the true "Demarcus Ware." But I had to make the decision to come see you; that was not easy, but it was my decision point that I will never forget.

So many people are lost and struggling every day. Those of us who have found solid footing and a foundation of emotionality owe it to others to share our wisdom and beautiful teachings. Dr. P, you are the most caring and insightful person I have ever met. Plus, you got swag, Dawg.

—**Demarcus Ware**
World Champion NFL Player

Chapter Eleven

BE THE CHAMPION OF YOUR LIFE

What little kid (boy or girl) doesn't love getting a new football or special toy for Christmas? Once it's opened from under the Christmas tree, the rest of the gifts doesn't really matter – being in Christmas pajamas doesn't matter. In my case, just throwing a new football, putting a spiral on it, running with that beautiful, brown leather ball and imagining the hours of joy to come is all that really mattered to me on Christmas morning. I always loved football. I got new footballs at Christmas, spent hours in front of the TV watching my favorite teams make plays that I honestly thought I could have done better – kicking field goals, punting, and making big defensive stops were my favorites. Celebrating the victories of my favorite team, I loved everything about football. If a friend came over, I'd automatically say, "Hey, let's go throw some passes." If my brother Danny and I were hanging out, it'd be, "Come on, Man, it's time to go throw some." Football was part of my life, my DNA, if you will.

It seemed that other kids in my class and around me got the advantage to play formal football with uniforms and helmets and all the gear, but not me. I guess I never even thought to ask. It wasn't until a good friend of mine named Brett Gordon, who was playing organized football, approached me and asked, "Hey, Man, why don't you think about coming out for our team?" I went to practice with him one day, and I watched, and the coaches came over to me and asked, "Hey, have you ever thought about playing?" "Yeah, it's funny you asked that because I was just going to talk to you after practice about that." I was about 11 years old then.

The kids on the team that I was watching were a year older than me, so I played up a year. But it really didn't bother me that much because I was big for my age and pretty advanced in strength. I think genetically we come from a good gene pool in my family, because I've always been one of the strongest players on all my teams, if not the strongest.

Anyway, that was the beginning of my football career, when I really started playing. I'll never forget the $50 it took to go out and buy my shoulder pads, helmet, football pants, and all the other gear. It was a very exciting time for me to really begin playing football. From day one, football really changed my life, not so much from the athletic standpoint, but from the leadership standpoint. Early on, one of the coaches singled me out, even though I came out late, about a week after the team had started. He singled me out as a person that could be a leader on the team.

"You know, I'd like you to be one of our captains," he said to me after one practice.

"Wow, okay," I said, rather surprised, but then had to ask, "What does that mean?"

"Well, you're going to talk to the team and motivate them. And as a matter of fact, tomorrow I'd like you to get in front of the team and talk to them about your goals as a captain and then as a team."

I'll never forget that because I remember going home and telling my mom that I had to come up with a presentation for our team. I was a year younger than these kids, and I was also a year younger in my grade. So essentially, I was two years younger than these players that I was going to be speaking to the next day – no sweat.

I'll never forget going home and getting in front of the mirror and preparing my speech like a true orator. I practiced to the mirror about how we could be a great team if we played together as a solid team and played for each other, how our performance would be even stronger. At 11 years old, I already knew those principles were the factors that made winning players and champion teams. Who knew that 40 years later I would employ those bits of wisdom as a performance psychologist in the NFL, NBA, MLB and corporations around the world?

The next season, I was again chosen as captain. By playing hard, playing within the rules, yet playing very, very aggressive football as a linebacker and then on offense as a running back and punter, I was recognized for my consistent performance and then called upon to speak and lead the team; that's how leaders are made. You have to play, fight, and win hard every day. High school football really empowered me that way and set a strong foundation for my future. Leaders are made when we are called upon for a duty that literally stretches us out of our comfort zone. It forces us to do things we have never done before and to still jump into it without a parachute, so to speak. Leaders are made when you volunteer to do something that you have never done before and then say, "Oh shoot. Between now and my delivery date, I better figure this out," then you do! That's when leaders are born!

I'll never forget that a turning point for me confidence-wise and as a leader in my high school career was the minute one of my teammates named Jim Hansen approached me in the hallway after our season was over my senior year.

"Congratulations on making All-City," he said as he approached me with a fist bump.

"What are you talking about?"

THE MOMENT LEADERS ARE BORN

"You made first team for All-City," he said.

"Wow, how'd you know?" I asked, curious.

"Well, it was in the newspaper this morning, and I read it," he said.

I ran and found a newspaper in the library and looked at it, and there was my name in print. I did make first team All-City linebacker. And that was the turning point for me because I was singled out as one of the best in our conference at my position. And it confirmed to me that I was doing the right things. The weight training, the nutrition, the protein shakes that I was drinking, the work on my communication skills as a leader on my team – it was all working. That was important for me going forward to really know that other people recognized this as well. It was rewarding to be recognized as a leader.

As a college freshman, I walked into my first college experience with zero expectations but with an attitude that I was going to play hard. I played linebacker, so I had decided I was going to go full-force, and that meant hitting people, and that's just what I wanted to do. I wanted to hit people on the field, play hard, have fun, and everything else would take care of itself.

Because of my full commitment and seeing myself as a leader in football, I was chosen to start in the middle of my freshman year. I was chosen over a senior, so it was quite an accomplishment and meant even more. It was challenging socially because as a freshman I didn't have a lot of friends on the team, and when we traveled it was more difficult because everyone else on the bus or plane was an upperclassman. It was worth the sacrifice, though, for how I was excelling athletically. I started to believe I actually did have a future in football.

After starting my freshman year, I was a starter from day one of my sophomore year and was picked to make some preseason All-Conference teams. That was quite an honor because I had earned that just from playing in my freshman season and had a really successful sophomore season to follow on. For those who understand the game, I led the front seven in tackles behind the line of scrimmage and quarterback sacks. We had a couple of seniors playing too, so it was quite an honor that I was able to perform at that level and hold my position.

The first turning point in my football journey was when I was named "All-Conference" in high school. The second turning point was when I started as a freshman in college. But the third turning point in my career was when, after the season, Head Coach Mike Friedman called me into his office and, extending me a large white envelope, said, "I got some other mail for you."

I thought it was from my parents or something like that, but he starts shuffling a stack of mail and handed me a couple more, large envelopes – one from the Dallas Cowboys and one from the Seattle Seahawks. I opened them right then and pulled out a typed letter addressed to me, Rick Perea. I'll never forget the Dallas Cowboys' letter: On it said, "Life with the Dallas Cowboys." At first, I thought, "Oh, okay. Dallas, they're sending me some stickers or something."

Coach smiled really big and said, "Well done."

"Coach, what does this mean?" I asked, still not clear.

"You're now on the radar screen of these teams, and now they're actively watching you and looking at you. Those are questionnaires that you need to fill out for them."

I went back to my townhouse, opened them up, filled them out as fast as I could, and sent them back in the mail. The Dallas Cowboys followed up shortly after; I got a package that had a license plate frame, decals, and books and pamphlets that boasted, "Life with the Dallas Cowboys."

It got me excited. And the same thing happened with the Seahawks. At this point, I began to realize how cool this was and how important my playing was. *Wow*, I thought, *These teams, after only my sophomore season, are really interested in me according to those letters that came within the packages.*

"We're very interested in you as a potential prospect and potential draft choice in two years to come, and we want to fly you out and test and measure you," they read.

That was the third turning point in my career that really helped me realize that I had something special and that football was really going to open up for me. I really want to speak to this because the brain is so powerful in the way we think and the way we perceive our circumstances. We know that thoughts lead to feelings, feeling leads to mood, and mood leads to behavior, which determines our performance. So, you see, at this point in my career, I really started to think, *Wow, I do have something special.*

I reviewed the dynamics that all played out to the sum of this: "You always just play hard. You're humble, you do your best and you hope for the best." But I also knew at this point that I had something that was different. In my sophomore year, I led the nation in sacks in Division II and was really starting to rack up some statistics that were very impressive in the world of football. I also led the conference in punting average and made all-conference at both positions. Now that is somewhat unheard of; making all-conference on both offense (punter) and defense (defensive end) during my collegiate career. But now that I had external confirmation and validation from the NFL, now that they were interested in me, this was really a turning point for me to boost my confidence and keep my leadership skills developing. All of this impacted me and motivated me at a deeper level, and I began to think of myself as a leader in many ways because now I also had proof and validation that others saw me as a leader.

I remember telling my girlfriend at the time, Tobie Snyder, that the Dallas Cowboys and the Seattle Seahawks were interested in me, and I'll never forget what she said and how she said it.

"So, the Dallas Cowboys know who you are?"

I said, "Yeah, they do." And it was a pretty cool moment as I took it all in. It was a salient moment to realize that I was actually on the radar screen of NFL teams. This was a turning point that really catapulted me not only as an athlete, but as a leader, because it gave me the confidence to lead because I knew others saw me that way. And as a result, I began to have even higher expectations for myself as a communicator and leader.

I didn't really even realize the magnitude it would have on my development as a leader and in helping me establish solid relationships with the coaches. As I mentioned in a previous chapter, I have one coach from high school, Coach Larry Tarver, who really had a huge impact on my life and still does to this day. As described, his family was in an automobile accident where his wife was seriously injured and had brain injuries and literally had to learn to walk and talk again. He has stood by her and been an exemplary role model to me. I also mentioned earlier in the book, at the college level, my defensive coordinator, Coach Bill Jacobs, was a huge motivator for me, an inspiration. He taught me leadership beyond anything I could have hoped to enjoy and experience, and at such a high level.

Then, in a very tertiary way, Coach Dan Reeves, head coach for the Broncos when I was a rookie with them in 1983, stepped in as a mentor to me. I was having some issues with keeping my head in the game. I wasn't sure if I wanted to play football anymore. I had some real doubts when I got to that level because there wasn't a lot of love, if you will, when you're a rookie, free-agent linebacker in the NFL; your kind of flying solo, a small fish in a big pond. And I was used to a lot of love, so I just struggled.

THE MOMENT LEADERS ARE BORN

I remember sitting down to talk with him, and he spent quite a few minutes with me, probably 45 minutes, which was a lot at that level. He said to me, very straight forwardly, "RP, once you quit once, you'll quit the rest of your life." I'll never forget that. I thought, *Well, if I do quit, that doesn't mean I'll quit everything. Maybe this is just not for me. Maybe it's just the NFL; it's not a fit for everybody.* But I never forgot what he said. I remember linking with him years later at the Broncos' facility when I was a psychologist and talking to him, I reminded him that he told me that quote, and I said, "It's been an inspiration to me my whole life because I've made sure I've never quit anything else besides the NFL." He laughed about that and said, "I am glad such a negative comment had such a positive effect on you."

The relationship you build with the coaches along the way is paramount in establishing a level of leadership. I have so many stories that I could share about conversations that have had that really inspired me to be a champion in life. One of the things that I think I've done is taken the experiences of teammates and of coaches that I garnered through high school, college, and pro levels to levels beyond the norm.

I even continued to make lasting friendships with teammates beyond the football field. For example, a few of the guys I met through my time with the Denver Broncos as a player were Greg Boyd, Larry Evans, and Rick Parros. I spent 13 hours shooting a McDonald's TV commercial in the mid-eighties with these guys; that experience really bonded us. Who knew it took 13 hours to film a 30-second commercial? But it made time for some great fun and bonding with these teammates. That experience created a lasting bond, and we are friends to this day.

We build relationships off of the football field, and my relationship with my Bronco teammates was paramount to me. After our careers, we continued to lift weights together at the gym. Larry and Greg even helped me with bodybuilding, and I helped them in their training, as well. Teammates stay tight, through the shared experience of football and from the camaraderie shared off the field too. Just recently, Rick Parros, a former running back for the broncos reached out to me after he heard me on the radio, and we have reconnected as well. Leaders do that – they honor relationships of their teammates. They don't burn bridges, they build them. For me this always meant that I stayed in touch with former teammates and coaches. This is key; many people simply "lose touch" and don't make that extra effort to reach out without any particular motive other than to say, "Bro, what up? How is the family?"

These friendships can potentially follow you through life. And after football they are so important because the average career is short-lived. Football players often must reinvent themselves for life. After I chose to walk away, I had to do that in a big way, too. I was veering hard away from football, but it was part of my core and my history, and I would soon learn how to leverage that to create a new career path.

As a defensive football player, you're always trained to attack. You're trained to be a warrior and not really process or think about pain or injury, whether received or delivered. There definitely was a transition after my position on the field. At the core of who I really am is a real innate need, in my DNA, to help people and heal people. Because of the pain and trauma that kept showing up in my life, it is really an important aspect for me to help and heal others.

I gained great insight from my football career experiences, from high school, through college, to the NFL, of what players actually go through. I knew early on and firsthand that there were a lot of us that needed help, and some of the work I do in my practice, even to this day, is with players like Julius Thomas, Ryan Harris, Brock Osweiler, Ryan Tannehill, Rick Parros, and others. I could go on and on. I'm working with these players presently to understand the mentality of the game, how it impacts our identity, how football shapes our perceptions, thoughts, and feelings, and what it demands of us as players, as well the personal cost of the sport. My personal experience definitely helped me as a psychologist today to process and understand how to help current players.

As a psychologist and a former player, one of the major things I did to transcend myself was to think outside myself. As a player you're always thinking about yourself as an individual, and even though you're a part of a team, it still was very self-oriented. We have a technique we teach called self-transcendence, which helps to address conceptual boundaries. It also means we go beyond ourselves; we shift the focus from ourselves to others, helping others and focusing on their work or what's important to them, meaning we think of the greater good. Stepping out of the self and helping someone else actually helps the self as well. We are wired to be givers, to offer love, to think of our neighbors more than ourselves. However, we often stray from this due to our societal norms of individualism, especially in the US. Through this giving concept, we actually receive great intrinsic rewards with bigger payoffs than when we serve the self. Leaders, good and great leaders, focus on serving others. Further, leaders are made when we transcend self and seek to serve others.

Leaders often have to reinvent themselves to stay in the game or keep one step ahead of the game of business. I certainly had to once I left professional football, which is a world all its own. The transformation from player to psychologist involved a lot of work, and that included the self-transcendence piece, shifting my focus from myself and my performance and achievements to others and their purpose, objectives, and goals.

As leaders this is so important, and the same concept applies. Passing this knowledge to other leaders helps them to thrive in organizations, teams, anywhere, really. When you focus on helping others, you empower the group, the team, the larger population of people that is much more powerful than the individual. This is done through finding value and meaning and by serving with kindness. Kindness is such an overused word, but kindness really means that your objective and goal is to treat people with love and care, with an open and generous heart, in a very respectful way, in a very loving way, and we can do that through many things, such as good deeds, through supporting others with their projects, thoughtful notes of affirmation, small tokens of encouragement, time and mentorship, even through playful singing and dancing to break up the monotony of challenges. I know that, for me as a former athlete, where both control and freedom of my physical being were important, one of the things that I love to do is to be very playful and even to sing and dance for brief moments of fun and relief. It puts everyone in a really great spot and elevates the mood – it's an excellent tension reliever and frees the mind, body, and spirit.

It actually has a psychological impact; we call that emotion of elevation, that's when you bring awe and amazement to an experience and express that to people, like, "Wow, this is amazing, and I'm in awe of that – that's incredible." Even our language and word choice help to elevate the mood of the environment, climate, and culture and thus impacts the results.

It was very satisfying to me to learn skills that would help alleviate stress and anxiety for those who had to perform – from football players to businessmen and -women, first responders, doctors, lawyers, engineers, or everyday people – seeing the need of how many had pain and anxiety right below the surface. The higher you climb, the greater the perceived stress and the expectation to consistently perform at your best. To compound that pressure, there are expectations for leaders and top performers to hide any stress while doing it – the expectation is to look like a million bucks and make it seamless to maintain the champion status.

Every year before the draft, we (NFL teams) would bring in the top 30 players prior to the draft. It was very obvious to me that most of these players had a good deal of emotional pain right below the surface, because I would ask a series of questions and it would illuminate the pain they were experiencing and bring it right to the surface. I knew I could help these players. It was important to me to help them; I had to work covertly because being a top player often meant you never truly let your guard down and shared. In general, people often look at pro football players as warriors, as tough guys, and it's really not okay to have or express emotional or psychological issues. It's very common for a player to walk into the training room and say, "I've hurt my knee or hurt my elbow," and a trainer will say, "Hey, jump up on the table. Let's take a look at it." But to walk into the training room or the office and say, "I'm really struggling emotionally," is not the "NFL protocol," if you will. Much more work and communication are needed in this area – and, I realize, not just on the football field, but in many industries and organizations.

Anxiety is the number one performance killer and the most unaddressed factor in the performance world, including athletics. A certain amount of anxiety (zone of proximal development) is good, as it helps us to perform and motivates us to reach higher, but it can handicap our high-performing athletes and many people and leaders who must perform at a high level. Going a little into the psychology of this conditional element might help you better understand. I believe teaching about the autonomic nervous system – both the sympathetic and the parasympathetic sides – is key to helping the performer understand what is really going on and to improve and regulate anxiety (see graph in Chapter 3 and at the end of this chapter).

What does the autonomic nervous system look like and what does it impact? The system automatically (hence autonomic) responds when the brain perceives a threat with the pituitary gland, releasing more adrenaline, which activates that sympathetic side, automatically. First, I want to delineate the difference between the brain and the mind: The brain is the anatomy, literally the physical elements – hypothalamus, hippocampus, pituitary gland, etc. Everyone who has a healthy brain has identical brain parts and systems. The mind, in contrast, is the brain plus input – education, experiences, and age, to name a few. As stated, when the brain perceives a threat, big or small, the pituitary gland automatically releases adrenaline that kicks in the sympathetic side of the autonomic nervous system. The results of this are increased heart rate, increased respiration, muscle tension, and narrowing of thinking. The parasympathetic side of that includes symptoms that are the opposite: lowered heart rate, calm breathing, relaxed muscles, and clarity of thinking. Helping people understand how to operate from that parasympathetic side is really vital to what we do as performance psychologists because elevated anxiety is the one factor that really harms or curtails performance both emotionally and physically. We identify the physical anxiety as somatic anxiety and thinking anxiety as cognitive (thoughts) anxiety.

In my transition from a player to psychologist, I realized the deep impact my work would have on other performance athletes.

THE MOMENT LEADERS ARE BORN

My former positions really opened doors for me to get into the NFL organization as well as major league baseball and the NBA. It was really helpful for me to be a former player as a psychologist in those three areas of pro sports because I had been an athlete and I knew what they might be experiencing. I knew the communication styles, the vernacular of the environment, the different taboos and approaches. I also now have the added bonus of travelling extensively and interacting with cultures from all over the world. It does help me when working with others from various backgrounds.

My connection to football and my personal relationships with people in the arena might have opened a lot of doors for me as a psychologist, but once I got in the door, I had to be able to demonstrate my leadership and my technical skills to truly help these players using my protocols and practices. So much of my experience with loss, with murder, with those different types of experiences, helped me reach a lot of these players, as well. Surprisingly, many players have also experienced loss and faced traumas in their own families. I can bring them self-regulation through leaving their comfort zone, feeling the pain, letting it go, breathing, visualizing, and so forth, until they are able to push past it or let it go.

Eleanor Roosevelt once said that you must "do one thing every day that scares you." I'm not sure I agree with the word *scare*, but I would say that we do have to leave our comfort zone emotionally and psychologically if we're ever going to grow and expand our horizons and our vision of who we are and where we hope to evolve. I train my clients to leave their comfort zone at least five times a day with the ultimate goal for them to be comfortable being uncomfortable. Once you're at that level, you're really not uncomfortable anymore. It's like the "face the fear and do it anyway" concept, but in this context it's "feel the fear, step into the fear, face the fear, and realize you are okay through it, and you are no longer full of fear." In psychology, we call this "flooding," meaning you flood yourself with the very stimulus that makes you anxious and you push through anyway. This experience cultivates a belief system that "if I can do that, face my fears and push through, then, I can do anything." It has been resolved. So, leaders are willing to get uncomfortable; they are willing to face the fear, stretch themselves, and grow to new levels. Leaving your comfort zone is a key component of being a champion of your life. Mediocrity is staying stagnant in place in what you do. Being stagnant means, you're not growing, you're not expanding yourself in any way, you are just complacent. One key benefit of leaving your comfort zone is that it brings you to a new and higher level and lends the ability to see things from a new perspective, including seeing things through other people's viewpoints. In life, we can be very ethnocentric and very egocentric. And when we're very centric to our own viewpoints, belief systems, attitudes, and values, then we do not expand the way we think, and it limits our sensitivity to others. But when you see things from other people's viewpoints, for example, you might say, "Wow, I hadn't thought of it from that perspective." Growth has occurred at this point, and you are now a stronger leader and an even more compassionate leader, because when you see things from other perspectives, you become more compassionate, which is always a desirable trait of leadership.

Further, I want to emphasize that growth occurs only when we feel some level of discomfort. When we're pushed to feel discomfort, when we feel pain, when we feel certain levels of anxiety, that is what fuels some level of awareness and growth. That's such a key component because growth doesn't happen without awareness, and awareness doesn't happen without discomfort on some level. You can consider it pain. You can consider it emotional or psychological anxiety, but growth really occurs when we feel discomfort. And the ultimate level of growth happens when our cells divide, for example, when we're growing and expanding in the physical realm. So, it happens that way cognitively and psychologically too in the form of new thinking pathways (neurogenesis).

So, in essence, what we say in my practice is to be a champion of your life and search for methods that stretch you to a level of discomfort; remember, a prerequisite of performance is to initially experience discomfort; then, and only then, will you begin to experience comfort being uncomfortable. You train the brain in a new way of processing. If you stay in your comfort zone, if you stay in that area that you have in your life that's really the same, the monotony of mediocrity, then that's just where you'll stay, you will never begin the trail from uncomfortable to comfortable when facing the same stimuli. So, you have to accept that there's going to be a requisite level of discomfort initially; physical (somatic), and thinking (cognitive), discomfort, perhaps both, depending on your endeavor.

To be a champion of your life is dramatically influenced by how you think; because how you think, will determine whether you're comfortable experiencing discomfort. I repeat: How you think will determine how comfortable you are experiencing discomfort; that's a key element I want to discuss because, like we said earlier, thoughts lead to feeling, feelings lead to mood, and mood determines behavior. As such, your thoughts are the performance foundation of the mental house you build. Whether you change the old furniture in the house one room at a time or move all the old furniture out in the whole house in one thought is up to your capacity to change, but at some point you have to be willing to change the old furniture in your mental house. For example, deciding to cut back on smoking cigarettes is changing the old furniture one room at a time; stopping smoking altogether in one day, like some do, is deciding to change all of the old furniture in one thought, in one day. Most people want to move away from pain. Most people don't quite grasp or understand the magnitude and the value of discomfort and how it can really propel us to be a person and leader beyond our own belief systems.

When I was getting recruited to play college football (at the time weighing 210), I had coaches tell me that, by the time I would be a senior in college, I would weigh 240 pounds. I can remember thinking, *There's no way. I don't even want to weigh that much as a linebacker.* These coaches had a vision and a mission beyond what I saw for myself, and they knew what it took to go after another human being on the football field. Come my senior year in college, I weighed 240 pounds. I had to leave my comfort zone to achieve this, but it was a key component for me to become a champion on the field. Go for it; experience the requisite discomfort and become the champion of your life.

Once I learned some of the techniques in Performance Psychology and I started to apply them decades ago, my performance went to a whole 'nother level. One great example is the victory with the Denver Broncos from 2015–2016, when we won the Super Bowl World Championship. There are a couple of stories that will always highlight my life in terms of that year and that experience. Ryan Harris, Demarcus Ware, Von Miller, and Brock Osweiler are champions on the field and were key to the Broncos' championship and to my interaction with the team, impacting this amazing victory.

Von Miller (outside linebacker) has always been a dominant player in the NFL since his rookie year, but when he came in to see me as part of my work with the broncos two thirds of the way through the 2015 season, he was looking for new ways to approach the mentality of performance and the post season leading up to the championship game. I taught him visualization and the technique of SIT, which is a protocol to use imagery and diaphragmatic breathing to ease anxiety which puts us on the para-sympathetic side of the autonomic nervous system. He admitted that it really took him to the next level and that it was a powerful point for him in his career because he had learned to manage his emotions going forward.

Victory, championships, the public spotlight, and the pressures from the game all can cause a person to lose their identity and their focus. Demarcus Ware was one of those players when I met him. He came to Denver from the Dallas Cowboys because he was looking for a new direction. He struggled for contentment and balance in his life. At times he had lost his focus. Working together, using the protocols of my practice, we were able to achieve breakthroughs on a new level. This helped him achieve a higher level of performance on the field and also find himself as the man he knew himself to be. He said that in many ways he was lost before he worked with me, that I helped him recapture himself and his life off the field, and this showed up to positively impact his performance on the field. He was able to rise up and be a better athlete and step into leadership as he was able to speak to his teammates and propel them to achieve more. He became an incredible leader on his team, which inspired the team for closer connection and greater performance. Many people think winning games and Super Bowl games is all about talent, and every NFL team has talent, but very few teams have the brotherhood and the social cohesion that it takes to perform at peak levels. Through Demarcus' experience and sharing it with the team and showing up in new ways for the team, this environment of brotherhood and cohesion was achieved, and their performance that golden day demonstrated the impact.

Demarcus Ware is also, in my opinion, the uncrowned MVP

of Super Bowl 50, because he also helped prepare Von, the MVP of Super Bowl 50, for that day on the field from the neck up. The physical part is important on the field, but addressing the mindset, the emotional health, and everything from the neck up is truly what wins games. Leaders lead by helping others perform their best; this creates the best outcomes. Leaders aren't always the ones leading from the front. Everyone on the team, everyone on the field, has an opportunity to lead for the win.

Sometimes there are setbacks that turn into set-ups. This was actually a factor leading to the Super Bowl championship. Brock Osweiler, our backup quarterback, was that player when Peyton Manning went down due to an injury and didn't play for seven games. Brock was the starting quarterback and went five-and-two in those games. That was more important than people might realize, because if we don't go five-and-two in those early games, we don't enter the playoffs, especially in the position to have home field, which truly gives the team leverage for the best possible outcome. Every team member plays an important role leading up to wins on the field, but these wins are even more important in setting up an optimal environment for the championship, which did indeed happen for the Broncos.

Brock Osweiler and Ryan Tannehill are probably the most astute student/quarterbacks I have had the honor to serve, and Brock translated his knowledge to the field and shared it avidly with his teammates. He and Tannehill were both great quarterbacks for the NFL and great students of mine; as I write this book, Tannehill was just named Comeback Player of the Year in the NFL. Both football pros believed in their transformations and what they learned during our time together so much that they brought it to other quarterbacks throughout the league, including when Brock went to Houston and then on to other teams in Cleveland and Miami. Brock worked with me the summer prior to the 2015 season, and we were able to put in place strong protocols and a good mental enhancement package for him that he activated to become a world champion player. To this day, he credits working with me as a key factor in elevating his career and thus helping him lead as a champion on the field for the Denver Broncos' Super Bowl Championship.

I like to be available for my clients as the need arises, but I knew Super Bowl was the big one. I could feel the adrenaline rushing through everyone's veins even after practice leading up to the game. So, I told all the players the day before the Super Bowl, "Hey, tonight if you guys hit a sticking point or something comes up, you know you got my number. Hit me up," And Ryan Harris, our starting left tackle, did just that.

He called me the night before and said, "Bro, having a hard time sleeping. I've never played in the Super Bowl, Man."

I could hear the anxiety and the tension in his voice. "Look, Bro, you're already a world champion; all you need to do is go out there and play it, play it out like you know how to do. The field is 100 yards long by 50 yards wide. That hasn't changed. It's still the same game. And you're still the same person, the same great player. You just need to do your deep breathing, your visualization we've worked through, and go out and play. But you're already a world champion."

The next day, he went out and did what he knew to do. He kept his focus. He knew who he was. He used the skills we practiced. And he did it. He led the team by performing like a champion, and as a result, the Denver Broncos became Super Bowl 50 champions.

It takes a large pack to support champions to victories like that; they are the instruments, the top dogs, but it takes a pack to inspire them to the vision to win and to see themselves as the winners they are. About two weeks after the Super Bowl championship, I got a call from Ryan Harris.

"Hey, Doc, can I come to your office? I'd like to talk to you for a minute."

He arrived and we met for a strong handshake and slaps on the back and celebratory cheers for the recent victory.

"Remember you told me to visualize the night before? Well, I visualized that Peyton Manning would hand me the Lombardi trophy, and I would hold it up into the sky and the confetti would be falling down all around me – that's what I visualized."

I smiled, very proud of him, and feeling so proud that he remembered everything we learned to prepare him for the game.

"Doc, this is going to sound crazy, but that very same thing came true. I was standing on the field, and all the confetti was coming down, and somebody tapped me on my shoulder, and it was Peyton Manning; he handed me the Lombardi trophy!"

He was so excited telling me, and I shared his excitement. "Oh man, that had to be so awesome," I agreed with him, so happy for his reality.

"And really what set that up is Peyton was holding it up, and then they wanted him to come to the podium and speak, and since I was the closest one to him, he turned and patted my shoulder and handed me the Lombardi trophy to hold for him. Doc, I visualized that the night before, and it came true," he said emphatically, evidently still hardly believing it had come to pass.

And I agreed with him, so pleased that he employed the techniques and that I was now sharing in his victory.

"This visualization piece is so powerful; it's just amazing how that came true," he was still going on about this amazing event. It was so powerful, not only because he had just experienced the results from his hard work, but because he had just been changed by the experience, truly transformed, and that changes a man's life forever and forges the champion within.

"Yeah, it doesn't surprise me one bit because that's what it does. It trains the brain to be prepared for success. Once you're out there in the theater, in the war, when live bullets are flying, when the rubber meets the road, the footballs are flying, the brain is fully prepared for that."

What a powerful outcome. These guys make up examples of being the champion of your life, but it all comes back to showing up as a leader – being uncomfortable, being transparent, being vulnerable, self-transcending, and playing to win, not just for yourself, but showing up as the best version of yourself for others. Demarcus did this with Von, Brock did this with the other quarterbacks, Ryan did this with his offensive line teammates, and I did this, bringing my best, for all the players.

Ask yourself the question, "How can I leave my comfort zone five times daily? How can I leave my comfort zone in small ways, and slowly in even bigger ways?" Because the more comfortable you become being uncomfortable, then you are going to stretch yourself, and you are going to grow as a person and as a leader. This is a prerequisite for top performance. Leaders embrace the hard work to grow and know that it will pay off in dividends - winning the Super Bowl of their life.

Chapter Twelve

HOW I HELP AND HEAL

Performance anxiety is a real thing, even for very seasoned performers in any field where the pressure and expectation of results are paramount. This anxiety can be triggered by many factors, both external and internal, including mindset and/or biology. While perceived anxiety is a real construct, there are protocols and practices to help address, manage, and regulate the anxiety so that it doesn't negatively impact the outcome of the performance. Ideally, these techniques will help a performer, like an athlete, surgeon, pilot, or anyone wanting to be their best version, face the anxiety head-on and release it to regain strength, confidence, and a positive mindset to achieve desired actions for success. It is important to understand that, when anxiety is percolating, your autonomic nervous system is at work activating primarily the sympathetic side which elevates the germane vitals, limiting your ability to reach your objectives and goals.

Anxiety involves the autonomic nervous system (referenced in Chapter Three and below), which is the governing body of the parasympathetic and the sympathetic nervous systems. When you understand these two aspects of regulating anxiety, you will have additional insight into what happens physiologically and psychologically when anxiety hits and paralyzes performers; that's why, in essence, we developed the techniques and the protocols that we teach at ThinkOne.

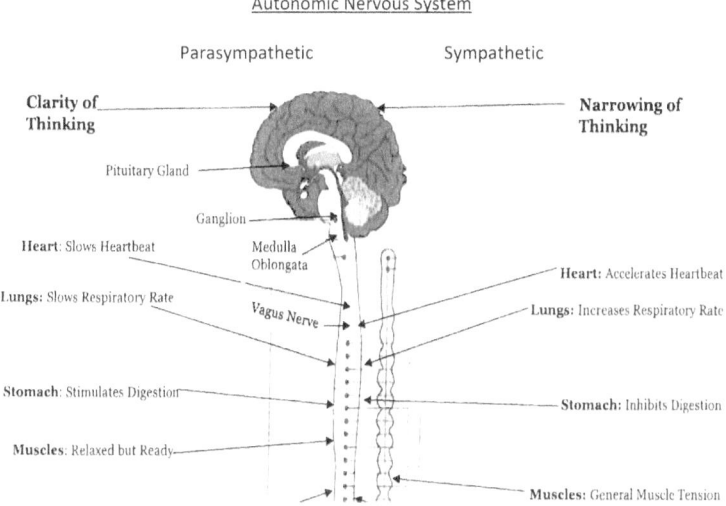

Many of our most effective practices and protocols are born out of teaching the Autonomic Nervous System and specifically how to remain on the parasympathetic side during performance. In fact, it would be safe to say, that I conceptualized ThinkOne when I was enjoying the fruits of clear thinking, little muscle tension and calm breathing: the parasympathetic.

ThinkOne was born out of an idea, not from a model. Nobody else in the world has a similar practice for performance athletes, high risk/high reward occupations, everyday people, champions of life; in essence, people wanting something better for themselves. For me, I was motivated to create a state-of-the-art facility and do something nobody else had done. I decided that if I was going to open a facility for helping and healing people and was also going to work with the best of the best, then I was going to create a facility as such. Early on, I knew I was a pioneer by creating this practice and could find no benchmark in my industry.

I was a trailblazer, willing to take a risk of thinking and creating differently, with unique modalities and practices in place, offering services that would treat the whole client: mind, body and spirit; hence, ThinkOne. We treat clients from any walk of life and give them hope; hope to recover, hope to heal, hope to fight (we literally give miniature boxing gloves to our clients to honor the fight, as well as to honor my brothers as boxers) and win like a champion.

Oftentimes when other psychologists come into my facility, they will say, "Wow, where did you think of all this? Where did you develop this?"

I'll say, "Look, I just wanted to help and heal; and be cutting edge." As I look into their eyes, I say, "We offer the best for the champions on the field and in the real world of everyday people who need it to reach their potential. I know because once, that was me. I had to face traumas and tragedies on my own, get out on the field and perform day after day, game after game, and it knocked me off the field and eventually out of the game I loved so much. These champions, my clients, deserve the best that I can deliver; its personal for me."

ThinkOne was additionally born out of an effort to serve with excellence; to serve all people. One of the reasons I need to offer the highest level of service is because, when I'm treating the top NFL quarterbacks in the world, when I'm treating the top major league baseball pitchers in the world, and when I'm treating the best basketball players in the world, they want the best psychologist in the world. And quite honestly, my philosophy is that, if I'm working with the best in the world, I need to be the best in the world at my craft and offer an eclectic set of modalities. Further, when the CEO, CFO, COO or everyday performers like you and me is a participant in one of our programs, they want the best for themselves too; as such, me and my team better be the best for them as well.

What we really aim to do at ThinkOne is train the brain (neuroplasticity) to think differently (neurogenesis) and to align the thoughts with the goals and objectives of the individual we serve. We don't really train the mind; we train the brain, and then the mind follows systematically. At ThinkOne we treat the whole person. What we've done is brought together several different practices in one facility. In the past, the chiropractor was on Third Street, the psychologist was on Fourth Street, the gym was on Fifth Street, the acupuncturist was on Elm Street, and so on.

What we've done is married western medicine, which is the empirical modern medicine that we use in America, with eastern philosophy. If you walk into our facilities, on the right side of the building you will find a focus on eastern philosophy, and on the left side of our office is western practices and services. We form a nexus with those two philosophies to unify under one umbrella at our practice, which we call ThinkOne. Through this mind–body philosophy, we really want to address the whole person, and through multiple practices and modalities, we can achieve this.

ThinkOne was born out of my goal and my effort to be cutting-edge in our industry, but also to reach people who had given up hope that *authentic* help is really out there. Unfortunately, our industry tends to have a stigma attached to it. As I travel the US doing my thing, I ask people informally if they have ever had mental enhancement or therapy related to thinking and/or behavior. I would say 7 in 10 are not pleased with, not only the results of their mental interventions, but the process of finding someone and perhaps most importantly, the relatability and authentic skills of their practitioner. While I always keep credentials at the top of my list for scrutinizing potential hires for ThinkOne, the most important characteristic(s) that I look for in a mental health professional is an engaging, light and warm personality. Trust is the most important element we can build with our clients and then connecting with clients through authenticity and real-world relatability is paramount to building this level of trust. While I believe I bring world-class competencies and acumen related to mental enhancement, what separates me from most is that I am a real person that exhibits humor, excitement, energy and appropriate emotion with my clients. As you read a sampling of my client's testimonials later in this chapter, keep this in mind: My number one goal is to build trust and connect with my clients. Once that is achieved, not only will we have more fun learning, but the mutual trust is an amazing platform for teaching protocols and giving them tools that will last a lifetime. It is not uncommon for my coaching clients to remain friends for years to come; something considered "inappropriate" in modern therapeutic climates and culture that merely treat pathologies.

Another reason I'm interested in being cutting-edge is because of the populations I work with. Let's go back to before I founded ThinkOne: I was a college professor, and I taught classes ranging from introductory psychology to adolescent psychology. I also taught sport and performance psychology, which is very specific to the topics covered in this book. I also taught neuropsychology, which comprises study of the neurological processes and how synapses and dendrites of the brain communicate with the central and autonomic nervous systems. My foundation was as a scholar and a college professor, both the learning of and teaching of various aspects of psychology. I was able to bring that over and translate it into my own practice of psychology to uniquely serve my clients.

One of the things that I was moved to do from the beginning

of opening my own practice was reach different populations. For example, I started working in major league baseball and in the NFL, applying my psychology skillset, while I was also a college professor; it quickly became apparent to me that I wasn't going to be able to be involved in both because I was missing too much class time. I was having a hard time grading all my papers, so I decided to focus solely on growing my clients and my ThinkOne practice.

My practice is called ThinkOne: The Behavior Design Specialists, which is highly niched and focuses on behavioral design for all. Behavioral design is an approach which means we can actually design our communication and our behaviors intentionally. We can shape our thoughts, so we are not influenced or shaped by our random, external thoughts. ThinkOne is a name that is characteristic and inherent of thinking, number one, like a very strong belief system, but ThinkOne also represents "one," as in "whole" – the whole body, the brain, the brainstem, spinal cord, central nervous system, autonomic nervous system, and all body systems that are all connected; ThinkOne.

Our approach is a holistic one. If we only treat the brain or the mind without the body, that's not holistic; in this case, we have only looked at one system and ignored the whole body. ThinkOne is representative of what occurs naturally in performance; it requires the whole mind and body to perform, thus the whole body and mind is addressed to accomplish whole healing, wellness, and performance.

The behavior design specialty is specific to designing our internal communication (intrapersonal) that in turn designs our behavior (interpersonal) every day. It's a powerful place to be when you know you can design your behavior via your thoughts, which will influence your feelings and in turn will influence your mood, which will guide your behavior and directly impact your performance every day. This is a powerful approach for leaders.

In my practice, we teach protocols and techniques of how to regulate anxiety and, more specifically, help a person learn how to stay on the parasympathetic side of their autonomic nervous system, which is paramount to performance. When you're on the parasympathetic side, the heart rate is calm, respiration is calm, muscle tension is very, very low, and then we have a clarity of thinking and decision making; hence, the probability for peak performance.

The opposite of the parasympathetic side is the sympathetic side, which is where anxiety and stress generally live. That's the side where elevated heart rate, elevated respiration, elevated muscle tension, and narrowing of thinking get triggered. If you think back to being in an argument with your spouse, a parent, or a friend, and you said something that you later regretted, something that was not really what you wanted to say, and then two hours later you caught yourself as you played it back in your mind and recognized that you wish you didn't say that, that's when you were operating in adrenaline and anxiety. Two hours later you calmed down and you were on the parasympathetic side, and that allowed you to expand your thought in terms of clarity, now having more thinking options. When you have narrowing of thinking, you have very few options. We discuss the autonomic nervous system and how that operates automatically because the pituitary gland releases adrenaline and automatically kicks in the sympathetic side, which is most familiar to us as fight or flight activity. Through specific protocols, we lead you to recognize, regulate, and let go of these cyclic patterns of thinking that can be destructive.

Back 5,000 years ago, it was an important stressor to have – "I may have to kill that saber tooth tiger to protect myself," or "I might kill that wild boar tonight to feed my family." Back then, we needed the autonomic nervous system to respond immediately. But today we do not need that immediate fight or flight response for daily living – perhaps still in emergency situations, but not daily, when it shows up to induce long-term anxiety issues. Today, in the psychological realm, we assert that stress and anxiety are self-imposed, largely depicted by perceptual values. For example, when the brain perceives a threat, large or small, the pituitary gland automatically releases adrenaline, which automatically activates that sympathetic side of the autonomic nervous system.

At ThinkOne, we have the real and authentic opportunity to regulate client's behavior and live on that parasympathetic side, where performance lives. I have helped numerous men and women, including professional athletes, astronauts, attorneys, engineers, businessmen and women. They struggle with things that are of utmost importance to their success and happiness. Through brief sessions and a highly reliable personality assessment that only a select segment of Ph.D.'s have access to, we are able to help them identify their core challenges, develop a protocol designed uniquely for them, and help them conquer the anxiety that is derailing them by training and educating them to operate on the regulated side of the parasympathetic.

This approach to health is critical for leaders. First, it addresses the whole being, but secondly and most importantly, is that it identifies what is holding you back from operating as your best and consistently delivering excellent results. In my practice, a check-up from the neck up can have you performing like a champion every time; day in and day out. Our programs are called Alpha Coaching, Couples Synergistic Coaching, 360, and 212, for obvious reasons.

Leaders make their health a top priority, and health includes physical, emotional, and mental health. At ThinkOne we also enhance human capital performance in organizations, from small organizations to large. One way of doing that is treating people individually, as teams, or organization wide. Leadership training, psychological skills training, and communication skills training are several ways we help people, or human capital as it is depicted in the organizational context. On a more organic or biological level, we also provide neurofeedback training. We train clients' brains through computer programs, which has led to a lot of research that helps people regulate the five major brain waves for behavioral optimization. In fact, the work that we do by training and relaxing the brain cultivated the birth of a subdivision of ThinkOne called the BrainSpa. The BrainSpa is literally that – a spa for the brain. From neurofeedback, which also provides a quantitative EEG, to Apha-Stim, the SOQI bed and the sensory deprivation tank. These applications were researched and implemented at ThinkOne to combine western and eastern principles at the core; the BrainSpa is exclusive and unique in the industry. Recently, a fortune 50 company had five of its top executives visit the BrainSpa at ThinkOne to invigorate and rejuvenate their leadership team. The feedback was unanimous: all of the members expressed they didn't know applications like the ones at the BrainSpa were even available. They cumulatively also said that they became more relaxed with our modalities then at any other time in their adult life.

Since the BrainSpa and ThinkOne are so unique and exclusive in their application, let's take a deeper look at the some of the modalities that make-up our core of holistic treatment at our progressive organization: Thermo therapy with the bio mat, which has amethyst crystals in it that, when heated up by a control board, create far-infrared rays and negative ions that help break down lactic acid and metabolize the blood at an accelerated rate to calm the central and autonomic nervous systems. Most people when laying on the bio mat are sleeping within 15-20 minutes, completely relaxed. Float therapy, or more technically known as the sensory deprivation tank, is extremely effective at regulating brain waves, returning us to a theta state, which is a calm, relaxed state right before sleep or after waking. It's an optimal level for learning and perception. In addition, cranial electrotherapy, which regulates the alpha brain waves by utilizing the device called Alpha-Stim, is also used with great efficacy for regulating anxiety, depression, and insomnia. I have had so many pro and amateur athletes and performers in general, buy this device after I treated them at the facility. The scientific proof behind this device is empirical and significant. In fact, one NFL executive had professed to not sleeping through the whole night in 20 some years. After one treatment of Alpha-Stim, he slept through a meeting at 7:00 am the next morning and immediately bought one for himself and his family. Further depicting our treatment applications with an eastern slant at ThinkOne are the Tibetan singing bowls, which we've adapted to our practice in the last two years. The Tibetan singing bowls have been very powerful in my practice to help people regulate anxiety and reduce acute and chronic anxiety – acute being short-term and chronic being long-term.

Our clients have many unique options to fit their comfort levels and their needs. The many modalities elevate our practice to a level that is unmatched for providing desired results. The client can expect true breakthrough with performance anxiety or just improve their performance from their baseline and return to balanced living with a renewed ability to achieve peak performance, regardless of profession or occupation.

The services offered deliver life-changing results. A few examples may lend insight: I was recently the keynote speaker for the Colorado High School Coaches' Association, which represents all sports.

DECISION POINT

Every time I give a presentation, I tell the people what we deliver in our facility. I talked about how we provide the neurofeedback and how it regulates the brainwaves and that it really can change people's lives. After my presentation, I had a coach from a small town in Leadville, Colorado come up to me and say, "Your presentation was amazing. I have never heard of this neurofeedback. I have a 14-year-old daughter that has auditory processing challenges and real socially driven challenges. I would like to come into your office and learn more about it."

When they first came to the office, she brought her 14-year-old daughter with her. Her daughter had a hoodie on and was wearing it with the hood up.

14-year-olds wear their hoodies, I thought, and quickly dismissed it.

After they left, the mom called me and explained, "Yeah, I just wanted you to see how she dresses and how she avoids social contact." The girl's mom said she was very impressed with our demonstration and the facility and she wanted to begin one of our programs.

We offer two different programs: 360, which includes everything in the facility except float deprivation, and the 212 program, which includes the float tank. It's a one-year membership at our facility and they have use of everything here. I'm explaining this to tell you that the mom was eager to enroll her daughter, but I had my reservations about how much she would actually benefit from the membership because of the distance from their home in the mountains to our facility.

Leadville is two and a half hours away without snow, and we were heading into winter with the probability of snowstorms. The family committed and followed through on our program, and the client's life was radically changed. She came out of her shell and learned techniques to help her thrive again. But most importantly, her brain was trained to process information in a calm collected way. She is now a college scholarship volleyball player leading an amazing life. There are numerous stories like this, random connections from the events where I speak, referrals from other clients, folks who have heard of us through someone and show up and their lives were changed.

We have offices in Denver, Colorado and Greenwood Village, Colorado, which is South Denver, as well as satellite offices in Miami, Aventura, and Fort Lauderdale, Florida. My clients fly in often to receive services from state-of-the-art modalities and from the smorgasbord of offerings we have to treat the whole person and allow them to heal, receive, learn, grow, and find the peace in their minds and bodies in order to live a life restored, refreshed, in balance, aligned with who they truly are at their core. They come to ThinkOne to rediscover themselves with the tools to perform their peak levels and have their brains trained in a unique and exclusive way and leave as the champions they are. Our services are so effective, we guarantee them in full. Your success awaits. The following renditions are a testament to the collective effort and impact we have at ThinkOne:

Client Testimonials: The True Healing and Help Realized Through Dr. P's Practice at ThinkOne and the BrainSpa:

Dr. P,

Thank you! Words cannot express gratitude for the help you have given Sammi and me both. Watching my daughter come alive again in the last two weeks exceeds all expectations we had upon our arrival. Sammi has gone from a sad, self-doubting teenager to a positive, upbeat, creative human being. Her light is shining brighter now than it ever has.

Personally, I am thankful for your gentle, loving, "kick me in the ass" approach to my healing. I have been in a low of lows the last year with no hope of pushing through.

The good days were so infrequent that I was tolerating the hopeless attitude.

I'm fighting back again. I want to live life again. I want to be happy and get back to the normal everyday life activities. You opened my eyes to what I was allowing to slip away.

The combination of coaching and neuro was truly what I needed, and still need, but the foundations and techniques are coming. I have a desire and a deep-rooted need to be here for my kids. The negative thoughts are still there, and [are] very strong at times, but I am realizing they pass. Just because I am feeling it now does not mean that they have to stay. The improvements I have felt in the last few days have me starting to feel a small bit like me again. It is starting to feel right.

The staff has been so supportive, loving, and welcoming. We are going to miss everyone. The unconditional, loving push for Sammi and me to [see] our own worth will be a lesson we will never forget. We won't let each other. Plus, I have a butterfly tattoo to constantly remind myself that my story isn't over yet and breaking out of the cocoon is only difficult if I say it is...

It takes courage, and the three wonderful human beings I created with Tom deserve the world. To them, their mom is the world, and you have pushed me to not only see that but feel it and start to live it.

Thank you from the bottom of my heart. ThinkOne will always hold a place in my heart.
Love, Dianna

✶✶✶

THE MOMENT LEADERS ARE BORN

Dr. P,

There are not enough positive words in the English language to express my gratitude for your time, expertise, and help. This letter will serve as a small token of my appreciation.

Before I met you, my whole life was spent in the red box. I never left my bedroom, didn't speak to anyone apart from my parents, and honestly believed I was doomed to a life of misery and failure. I didn't think anyone could help me. From the moment I first stepped into your office, I knew there was something different, something special about the way you did things. A small glimmer of hope had started to storm.

Not once did you tell me I was mentally ill, depressed, or that medication would dictate my happiness. You told me things about yourself that no other psychologist on this planet would share with me. You showed me how my brain works and why it was behaving the way it was. You taught me the science behind the behavior. Never before has a psychologist made me feel genuinely good about myself and [made] me think that this is something I can control. I cannot say thank you enough.

I know that the techniques you have taught me will forever be engrained into my daily routine. SIT will be my morning brain fuel and will also be my go-to method of anxiety relief. I will live my life in the green box with a "F@$% it" attitude and an autonomic nervous system that functions parasympathetically.

Most importantly, you taught me not to care what those that don't matter think about me. You showed me that it's okay to dress in the clothes you want to dress in, wear the jewelry you like, and to just be whoever you want to be.

DECISION POINT

You haven't just been a psychologist to me, you've been the first friend I could truly confide in and know that you will not judge me but help me.

I hope to see you again in the future and to hear from you.
Yours sincerely,
Josh D., Client of ThinkOne

Here is a rendition from a client who was at the end of her rope when seeking help in the mental health field. Notice in her rendition her depictions are more about connecting and appreciation than psychological protocols. We somehow get those mixed up in the level of importance in the realm of mental health.

A Rap After Freedom

Dr. P here teachin a lesson
Just like my teacher did but
They wasn't a blessing
We talking bad and maybe
Good and just a lil bit down in
The hood Flexin at all em hater
With Ice head to toe

He talkin bout winnin the day
But all I could remember
Was how good he became
Thanks to Dr. P
I'm free minded with slang
Thinkin I don't give a F@#$ what
People gotta say

THE MOMENT LEADERS ARE BORN

He may bougie but he coo
Bracelets line his wrists
Asks too many questions
You might just get the list

He hella dope but he cares
Gotta mind full of passion
But understands what it like to
have issues, and be honest,
He responds fast
So don't be scared if you think
He aint with it
But he the Shit
So of course he be with you
Even when you've had it

He taught me to live
Like no one else could
And even brought me some
Rappers delight
In the goods
Showed me how to be myself
Around the people I love
Even if they hate
It doesn't cause me pain
I brush it off my shoulders like
It ain't nothing
Cause at the end of the day I'm
Just lovin

We shape our thoughts and
We ain't depressed
Keep a good mind and I'm on
The way to success.

Addie L.

✷✷✷

Dr. P's Eclectic Background and How that Impacts His Practice

Although I am predominately of Spanish and Italian descent, I do have about 10–12% Native American running through my veins. To be specific, I am from the Navajo Nation and the Sash Dine 'e Clan, otherwise known as the bear people. I honor my clan by the jewelry I wear (see picture; black bear claw in large bracelet) and the intuitive and clairvoyant ways I carry and express myself in my life.

For example, as a psychologist and member of the Society of Indian Psychologists (SIP), I use my intuition, clairvoyance and perceptive values to a great extent while helping and healing my clients. I was deemed a "healer" by a great Navajo woman who is a tribe and clan healer. Although she wishes to remain anonymous, I have been empowered by her acknowledgment of my gifts (clairvoyance and intuition), which fall into the human behavioral realm.

These eclectic traits actually make my helping and healing properties much more divergent, ataraxious and most importantly, effective in applying this wisdom and knowledge. In fact, *Meta-Psychology* recognizes clairvoyant psychology as "knowledge of information not necessarily known to any other person, not obtained by ordinary channels of gathering information or data," (Myers, 2014).

As such, my knowledge, skills, and abilities (KSAs) of the healing principles of my Native tribe and clan, married with the eastern and western methodologies I employ, make me unique in the field of American Psychology and help me to better serve my clients. Many of my clients featured in this book speak to my unique and idiosyncratic approach to helping and healing, and the fact that they have never met anyone quite like me or been exposed to the mix of practices and modalities employed is a significant testimony to ThinkOne and its divergent climate and culture.

This supports how powerful emotional, psychological, and physiological healing can occur when clairvoyance and intuition are blended into traditional western and eastern methods such as those offered through my practice like the Tibetan singing bowls, crystals, water modalities and energy psychology; pure ataraxy.

My diverse heritage positions me to see people through a unique lens of helping and healing. Simply put I love people. My passion and compassion places me as a mental health professional that is at the core, a messenger. A messenger of help and healing. I message the intangible, by which, the unavailable cannot deliver.

Black Bear Claw Jewelry –
A Symbol of Dr. P's Native American Heritage

Chapter Thirteen

PROTOCOL PRINCIPLES FOR ALL LEADERS

One of the unique protocols we use at ThinkOne is a tool kit of ready-made techniques for clients to use on the go. They have such significance and great impact for our clients, I wanted to provide them here for you to apply in your own life. The ThinkOne protocol cards, 34 in all, are applied to clients per their specific needs during a performance program as one of the intensive protocols available to achieve their success. The protocol cards were designed to be cues and easy-to-implement tools for our clients to focus and apply our unique content to their lives from anywhere. While also available electronically, they are tangible, tactile, and observable cards to remind our clients that learning performance cues are readily available when needed. In fact, we suggest and provide our clients with transparent card organizers to keep in their ThinkOne notebook that is also provided by ThinkOne upon the inception of our Coaching/Performance programs. The notebook keeps our cards and handouts organized in a uniform and sequential fashion.

Our performance programs chronicled below are comprehensive, evidence-based, and include western, eastern and some Native

American philosophies and methods that employ Performance Psychology practices and protocols. Cognitive Behavioral Therapy (CBT) and Rational Emotive Behavior Therapy (REBT) are utilized. These two methods are person-centered and emphasize engaging human connection, communication, and behavior.

First, to better understand the principles in the coaching protocols, you might like to have an overview of our three performance coaching programs. It might help you better frame how the leadership principle cards are integrated.

Our Four Performance Coaching Programs:

Alpha Coaching/Counseling:

This program is for the performer (in all of us) who wants to utilize progressive, cutting-edge techniques and practices in a coaching format. Life, career/occupational, and sport performance protocols are taught and discussed. The client walks away with "tools in their toolbox" so they are equipped to take on daily, weekly, or occasional challenges; we all face life challenges at times. After 12 to 15 sessions, a client is equipped to deploy newly learned skillsets, which can be expressed as knowledge, skills and abilities. A client is coached to express their best version consistently in both life and business. This program also includes a very reliable and valid NEO personality assessment administration and interpretation that will add a wealth of data for the client as well as data that is utilized to custom tailor a program for delivery.

Couple Synergistic Coaching/Counseling:

This package is for the couple who desires significant improvement in their communique and behavior through mental enhancement practices and protocols and Progressive Relaxation Techniques. This plan does include the administration and interpretation of the NEO personality assessment for depicting accurate behavioral tendencies for each individual. With great effort, energy and attitude the couple should expect profound change and discover congruency in their relationship. In approximately 15 couple sessions and 3 individual session each, the couple can expect profound change in communication and behavioral tendencies.

360 Performance Program:

This program is for the performer who wants to combine coaching and neurofeedback that regulates the five-major brainwaves for optimal communication and behavioral performance. It includes all the aforementioned practices above in the Alpha plan plus a full round of 30–40 treatments of neurofeedback (please see our website at ThinkOne4you.org for full data and information).

212 Performance Program:

This is our premier performance program. It includes all of the aforementioned programs above (excluding couples coaching) as well as unlimited float therapy in our Denver Facility. In effect, the client who signs up for this program, has a one-year membership at ThinkOne and can utilize all of our modalities and practices employed at ThinkOne.

Performance Protocol Cards

The following principles and protocol cards can be applied to most life situations. The content on each card is designed to be developed by one of our certified professional coaches. Ideally, we recommend you schedule a visit of our premiere facility and allow us to introduce you to our unique, world class practices and our professional staff. Let us discuss how you can best use these principles in your daily life and create a plan to live your life at 212° every day.

Following is a sampling of our performance protocol cards. Please review them, meditate on them, and apply them in your daily routines for improved mindset and performance. Feel free to reach out and share your success stories or if you need further feedback applying them.

LEADERSHIP/FOLLOWERSHIP

* Big '5' Approaches
* Followership Interdependence
* Followership Consent
* Followership Empowerment
* Leadership / Environment Fit
* Power & Influence of Leadership
* Power Sharing in Planning Change

MINDFULNESS PROTOCOLS

* Thoughts Are Not Facts
* Calm, Clarity, Freedom
* Moment by Moment Awareness
* Recognizing Bodily Sensations
* Accepting Uncomfortable Thoughts
* Sensory Processing
* Compassion Promotion

EMOTIONAL INTELLIGENCE

* Awareness & Perception of Emotions
* Impact of Emotions on Performance
* Emotional Regulation Leads to Better Outcomes
* Inability to Manage Emotions at Root of Most Performance Failure
* Difference Between Good & Great Performance is EI

ORGANIZATION PROTOCOLS

* Leadership / Followership
* Communication: Interpersonal
* Motivation: Intrinsic / Extrinsic / Achievement
* Roles: Acceptance / Compliance / Adherence
* Self & Team Efficacy (Confidence)
* Cohesion: Task / Social
* Goals: Outcome / Process

SIT PROTOCOLS

* Diaphragmatic Breathing

* Imagery (3 Types)

* Positive Self-Talk

* 3-5 Minutes in AM & PM

* Individualized Techniques Throughout the Day

GREAT 1 DAY

* Shift in Focus to 1 Day
* Minimal Impact of Yesterday
* Minimal Impact of Tomorrow
* Energy Centered on 1 Day
* Block out external factors
* Fosters All-In Mentality

EXERCISE THERAPY

* Reduces Anxiety & Depression
* Exercise & Mood Relationship
* Exercise & Well Being
* Exercise & Personality & Cognitive Functioning
* Exercise & Mental Alertness
* Exercise as Adjunct to Therapy

PARENT PROTOCOLS

* Reward Process Not Outcome
* Always Talk Positive About Team / Coaches
* Ride Home: Two Compliments; No Questions
* After Game: Let Them Come To You
* Blended Family: United, Consistent Routines
* Be A Soft Landing Place (Parent)
* Stable Home Environment

ENERGY PSYCHOLOGY

* Tapping, Accupressure, & Touch Therapy
* Bio-Energetic Patterns
* Disruption in Mood Driven by Body
* Six-Step Integrative Model
* Meridian, Chakra & Biofield Interventions
* Neuro & Electro Physiological Processes

COMFORT ZONE

* Willing to Experience Discomfort
* Leave Comfort Zone 5X Daily
* See From Others' Viewpoint
* Growth Occurs When We Feel Discomfort
* A Prerequisite of Performance is Discomfort
* How We Think Will Determine Comfort/Discomfort

SPIRITUALITY

* Prayers that have Cultural Meaning & Value
* Chants that have Cultural Meaning & Value
* Songs that have Cultural Meaning & Value
* Stories that have Cultural Meaning & Value
* Culturally Relevant Practices & Norms
* Animals as Powerful Metaphors; e.g., Buffalo

SELF TRANSCENDENCE

* A Shift in Focus From Self to Others
* Overcoming Limits of Individual/Self
* Finding Value & Meaning in Kindness
* Playful; Good Deeds; Singing & Dancing
* Produce Fruit in Others Life
* Emotion of Elevation: Awe; Amazement

LOCUS OF CONTROL

* **Internal Locus of Control**
  * You Have Control
  * Less Influenced by Others
  * Sense of Self
  * Physically Healthy

* **External Locus of Control**
  * Blame External Forces
  * Credit Luck for Success
  * Feel Powerless
  * Don't Trust Change

AUTONOMIC NERVOUS SYSTEM

* **Sympathetic Nervous System**
  * Increased Heart Rate
  * Increased Respiration
  * Increased Muscle Tension
  * Narrowing of Thought

* **Para-Sympathetic Nervous System**
  * Decreased Heart Rate
  * Decreased Respiration
  * Decreased Muscle Tension
  * Clarity of Thought

CHOICE

* **Purposeful Thoughts a Choice**
* **Random Thoughts Not a Choice**
* **We Shape Our Thoughts**
* **Everyday/Morning We Choose**
* **Everything in Life a Choice**

Chapter Fourteen

WINNING YOUR OWN SUPER BOWL

Everyone has a moment, and maybe several moments, in their life when they must make a decision. They decide to accept something, reject something, embrace something, or adapt to something. But there are these moments when we have that decision point when we literally say, "Hey, this is never going to happen again," especially, if it's a negative experience, or, "This is the reward I needed to help catapult me to that next objective, that next goal, that next level of growth I've been reaching for."

These are those moments when you must make a decision. Whether athlete or attorney, astronaut, businessperson or mom or dad, we all arrive at that moment when we must make a decision to meet the challenges of life. And the decisions lead to the outcomes that we're searching for. But the thing I want you to remember is that there is a whole psychology to making decisions and shaping your thoughts, because whatever your thoughts are will influence the decisions you make. And whatever thoughts you have will lead to your feelings, and your feelings will lead to your mood, and your mood will lead to your behavior, and ultimately your performance.

I mean, think about this from a simplistic level. When you're in a good mood, how do you perform? Generally, in life you perform well when you're in a good mood. Your emotions are elevated. You're in awe of things. You're on the parasympathetic side of the autonomic nervous system. Oxytocin and dopamine are being released in the brain which are bathing you in the pleasure centers of the brain. But those decisions come from your thoughts and how you shape them, or don't shape your thoughts. We get to shape our thoughts every day. I mean, some people think we're the passive recipients of thoughts leaking into our heads. No; we get to shape those.

Oftentimes decisions are made, and it takes us into a new frontier, a new horizon, a new universe, a new stratosphere that we haven't embarked on before and that we must strive to reach every day. That's why the decision point is so important, because that's the moment that leaders are made. You could be a leader your whole life into your 40s and 50s and be an organizational or a business leader, but let's say you haven't been a leader in other areas of your life – your fitness life, your financial life, your relationships– and you haven't mastered how to shape your thoughts yet, so all these years you've been performing from a deficit or fear base. You are not alone; many people do, but now is your moment to decide to live differently, to step it up, to become a leader in all areas of your life.

I've talked to several hall of fame quarterbacks in the NFL, for example, who have told me they operate from a fear base. When you operate from a fear base, you will not perform to your true potential. With a fear-based attitude, maybe you perform at 70–75% of what you are capable of, but you'll never be a true 100% version of you if you are operating from a deficit-based perspective.

While we talk about the moment leaders are born, I want you to understand that leaders are made on different levels. We have occupational leadership. We have sport leadership. We have fitness leadership. We have our family, our micro leadership, our macro leadership. So, leadership happens throughout our lifespan, often in different areas, and ideally comes together when we are reaching the best version of ourselves and towards personal growth to achieve high-reaching goals.

My moment of leadership came when I was playing football and my first coach asked me to be a captain and to speak to the team. But I've been faced with moments where I've had to make decisions to take on a leadership role and to step into higher levels of leadership. I mean, becoming an entrepreneur is a decision. Instead of working for someone else or working for a university or corporation, I had to take a risk and commit to that leadership for myself, my family, my staff, and for others.

I want us to understand that we become leaders in a moment sometimes. It doesn't take a semester; it doesn't take a year; it doesn't take a multitude of years. It can be in just a moment where we decide to be a leader, as opposed to a passive recipient of information. The psychology of leadership is that we understand that trauma and tragedy really are the fire that forges the iron. In fact, if you show me somebody who's been through some trauma and tragedy and they've been able to turn that experience into a positive, that's because they were in that fire and chose to become *more* as a direct result of their experiences.

I've often said that if my brother Danny was not murdered when I was 7 years old, I would've probably lived an average life. I really believe that. I would've lived a pretty run-of-the-mill life and kind of coasted through most of my experiences. Probably achieved a few things, but I never would've shown up big like I have, reaching for more. Since then I've always felt like I had to be a great football player, a great student, a great speaker, a great author, a great father – never just show up and see what happens, in complacency and mediocrity. And I'm still currently working on being a great partner, a great person, and a great friend. These are all very important roles to me. And when they're important, we are willing to make the decision to be a leader in those special areas too.

But see, for me, the watermark was at seven years old when murder showed up at my front door and I had a decision to make. I had a decision to make at 7, and again at 8, and 9, and 10, and really every day. How am I going to comport myself? How am I going to lead my life? Am I going to be a victim or rise to be a champion? I could have thought, *Oh, my older brother was murdered*, so therefore I have this deficit base, deficit way of thinking, and "play the victim role." Or I could show up big in life and look for opportunities to help others that have been through similar experiences.

Ironically, I think it's interesting that to this day, I feel like I attract people in my life that have experienced loss. I feel like I attract people that have experienced trauma and tragedy because I have. It's a beautiful attraction because, through sharing and giving to others, that's when we self-transcend. It's not about us, it's about others. It's about giving to others, sharing with others, being all we can for others that will truly help us reach our true potential in life. So, for me that's paramount; that we give to others, and we make that an important part of our life.

I think about my dear friend, Sandy Clough, and we've mentioned in this book about his son Ryan's suicide. When I look at what Sandy shared for this book, his story and the poem he shared, it's just touching to me because I'm a father. I'm a father of four, and I can only conceptualize what that must feel like to lose a child in that way. When I read his contribution, Sandy grew another 10 feet tall in my eyes. He's a very dear friend. He's a beautiful human being, one of the best in the world at what he does for an occupation as a sports radio personality in the Denver area. How reflective he was to share about the personal tragedy of losing his son, Ryan. As a psychologist, as a man, and as a father, I have a completely new appreciation for Sandy.

Since he's written that piece, I'm drawn to him and endeared to him even more, drawn to having coffee with him, sending him a simple text or an emoji of a star or a thumbs up or a heart so he knows how much I love him, because all of us are terminal in this world, and we can all use a little more love and support and encouragement.

I must give that credit to a dear friend of mine, Paul Newell. I was recently at his father's funeral, who I knew growing up. Paul, who is a very eloquent speaker himself, got up in front of the congregation and gave his father's eulogy.

"We often hear that cancer patients are terminal. And some of them are." He said, in front of us all, "You know, we're all terminal. We're all going to pass away. We're all going to die. None of us are getting out of here alive." And you know, he's right. So, if we frame our lives from a perspective of, I'm terminal, I am going to pass away at some point, I think that it helps us in terms of our motive for living and our kindness and compassion to others. As the saying goes, everybody dies, but not everybody lives. I challenge you to take inventory and decide to truly live.

The graveyard is the richest place on earth because so many dreams, hopes, and fantasies about what we could have been or could have accomplished have gone to rest in the grave. Don't die with your dreams still in you. Choose today, your decision point, to work tirelessly until they come to pass; choose to show up to be the leader you were born to be. There are so many people who want to write a book but didn't, and now they rest in the grave, so many people that wanted to become a doctor, a lawyer, or a pilot but didn't do it, and now they rest in the grave, people that wanted to say, "I love you" to a certain person but didn't, and now they rest in the grave.

So, all the things that we don't do, that we don't strive to do, that we don't search to do, like Eleanor Roosevelt said, "Do one thing every day that scares you," these become the things you must do. And I would further say, "We must do something every week that challenges us, every year that stretches us, every decade that changes us, that personally grows us and helps us be who we're supposed to be."

To quote a good friend of mine, former professional football player Julius Thomas, "You know, I want to skid into my grave with nothing left. I've used all my love. I've used all my hope. My body's used up – everything. I've given everything I have."

I love that. It's beautiful. Really that's the way it should be when we live life and live to love; then and only then can we truly maximize our performance as leaders. And that's the moment that leaders are born, the moment when we make the decision to fully live and give it all we've got. We have the courage to make the decision, we just have to make it and walk it out, without doubt. There are people who run away from decisions. They run away from challenges. They run away from opportunities. Self-sabotage is a very common coping mechanism when feeling anxiety. I'll repeat that: Self-sabotage is a coping mechanism for many people who feel anxiety. Making a decision that leads to leadership is the opposite. When you own and take on the opportunity to become a leader in the face of trauma, in the face of tragedy, that's when you will truly, truly have an opportunity to maximize your potential.

So, if you've been through trauma, and you've been through tragedy, and you've been through trials and tribulations that have stretched you, consider yourself blessed and consider yourself possessing a unique opportunity right now for the best and greatest decision of your life.

So here's my challenge – and the challenge must be met by you every day – that every single morning that you wake up you have an obligation to yourself to make a decision that you are going to be great for one day. You see, that's all you must decide and do – be great for one day, today, this one day.

In mindfulness, we talk about being present in this day, this moment. We talk about not letting yesterday take up too much of today. Don't let tomorrow take up too much today. Be present. Be where your feet are. The ultimate level of that is being great for one day, right where your heart and your feet are and where your life is happening, for one day, and that day is today. It's not tomorrow. It's not yesterday. It's today. And when you take it and frame it as one day, then you can give everything you have into that day.

I often have said this when I was a college professor before I walked into class, whether it was with 150 students or 15 students. Before I walked into class, I would say to myself, "I am going to color their world for an hour and a half today. My energy, my passion, my vernacular, my pronunciation, my enunciation, my knowledge base, and my thirst for life are going to color their world for an hour and a half."

So, I have a choice. Am I going to be average? Am I going to be good? Or am I going to be great? I have a choice. It is a choice to show up as average, as good, or as great. I get to choose that.

I don't have to call my mom in the morning and ask, "Hey, Mom, what percent should I give today?"

"80%, Son?"

"Okay, thank you." No.

I don't have to call my husband, my wife, or my girlfriend and ask, "Hey, Hun, what percentage of myself should I show up as today?"

"Oh, 72%."

No, I get to choose it. I get to choose how I color that delivery system for this one day. That's my choice. It's what I get to uniquely decide. And that is beautiful because when I choose to be great, I'm influencing others. I'm self-transcending. It's not about me. It's about me being great for one day for them, not for me, but for them. I am now role modeling and serving and excelling and leading. We have that choice every day. And if you stop and think about it, everything in life is filled with moments like that, choices. If I'm down and I'm depressed, aside from having a brain chemistry imbalance, I'm choosing to be down. If I'm up and fired up, loving the day, and embracing the day, it's because I chose to be that way.

Remember Tiffani's sister, Lexy, from Chapter Nine? Do you think when Lexy woke up that morning, she knew that was her last day walking this earth? I don't think so. Do you think Tiffani knew that was her little sister's last day? No, she didn't know. But it can happen at any time. This life that we know here can be taken from us at any moment. The rug can be pulled from underneath our feet. And then what are we left with? We're left with the hope and the dream that we lived the life that we set out to, that we left a lasting legacy of leadership and love.

My mom had one year of college education, a notable education for a female back in those days, but she was wise beyond the classroom and gave me powerful advice and wisdom. She said, "You know, Rikki, there's two types of people that die. The first kind is the person that knows they're going to die. They know they're passing away. It could be from natural causes, it could be from unexpected causes, but they say, 'Wait, God. Don't take me yet.' They beg. They plead. They're holding onto the curtains. They won't let go. 'Don't take me yet. I haven't climbed that mountain. I haven't told her I loved her. I haven't done this. I haven't done that. Wait.' And then the other kind of person that passes says, 'You know, maybe I didn't do everything I wanted to do, maybe I didn't climb every mountain I wanted to climb. I'm sure I missed telling someone I loved them, but, oh God, I'm going to tell you what, I have lived my life. I have lived my life to the fullest, so please take me."

I liken that bit of mom's wisdom to the Julius Thomas method – "Man, I skidded in here, Dawg. I skidded in here like I gave it everything every day."

And believe me, there are days where maybe it's not 100% or fully boiling at 212°. Maybe you're at 208° or 209° of performance. But don't show up at 170°. Don't show up at 160° and just slide in or coast through life, because that's a choice. Remember, all you must do is be great for one day, and that's today; that one day is today.

When you break it up and chunk it up by day by day, it's easy to be great for a day – just one day. You're going to go to sleep tonight. You're going to get the rest. The muscles are going to get fortified. The neurons are going to get strengthened in the brain. And then you wake up the next day and say, "Let's go! Let's live life today (1 day) to our true potential."

And through shaping your thoughts intentionally, you will live "one day, every day," because that'll influence how you feel, and that'll influence your mood, and that'll influence how you behave, and that's ultimately how you perform.

I want to really encourage you to understand your decisions are influenced by your thoughts. I want you to make the decision that's going to help you become a greater leader in your life. Oftentimes people don't consider themselves leaders, but everyone walking this earth is a leader – if only of their life. And a leader gets to choose how they show up every day.

All you must do is be great for one day, one day, and then, yes, it starts all over again the next day. Great for one day. Make that choice today. Make that decision so you can become born again as a new and different leader, even in the face of trauma and tragedy, and use it as an impetus from the fire that you've been through. That's what forges your iron. That's what's going to make you stronger, better, faster, more of a great communicator, great in relationships, great as a parent, great as an athlete, because you've been through the fire and you made a decision for one day, today, and for every day. We're all in this together. Let's lead and love and change the world, together. It's time to reinvent yourself and emerge as the leader you were born to be. This time, it will be the best comeback play of your life.

It was already decided in that first moment, decades ago, when facing the hard moment of life, the point of decision, that the real decision was made. In that moment when there was no breath, that moment of realization and death, a champion was born. In that moment, that decision point, a leader was born for life. And he went on not only to champion his life, but to help a league of world class athletes and champions garner the world football championship in the 2016 Super Bowl. His decision, at his lowest point, the moment that could have changed his life and claimed his dreams forever, made all the difference, to himself, to his family, to world champions, and to leaders like you and me, because he made a higher choice in the sliver of space in that moment in time. Now the choice is yours; this is the moment true leaders are born. What decision have you made to choose between championship victories and a life lived at

212° and anything less than the life you were born to live? This is your decision point. From this moment on, choose to embrace life at 212° and embrace your dreams for the win. Do it today – for just a day. You were born to be a champion. Go win the Super Bowl Championship of your life. You have faced your decision point, and you are ready for the big game of life and the bigger wins ahead.

And know this: if you need help or a nudge, call me, text me, tweet me, or email me. Trust and belief are foundational to Love; I trust you and I believe in you. Therefore, I love you! No, I am not *in* love with you, but I truly love you because to read this book and all its authenticity and core content, you are my kind of soul. Yes, I love you, believe in you, and trust you. Now, go champion the moments of your life and run for the victory!

BIBLIOGRAPHY

Statistics (Ch.6): Office of Adolescent Health. (2018, November 15). United States Adolescent Mental Health Facts. Retrieved from https://www.hhs.gov/ash/oah/facts-and-stats/national-and-state-data-sheets/adolescent-mental-health-fact-sheets/united-states/index.html

WSJ article (Ch. 6): Abbott, B. (2019, October 17). Youth Suicide Rate Increased 56% in Decade, CDC says. Retrieved March 30, 2020, from: https://www.wsj.com/articles/youth-suicide-rate-rises-56-in-decade-cdc-says-11571284861

C. S. Lewis Quote (Ch. 6): Lewis, C. S. (2016). *A Grief Observed*. London: Cross Reach Publications.

Song lyrics (Ch. 6): *Love is the Answer*. (n.d.).

Bible verse (Ch. 6): Isaiah 55. (n.d.). Retrieved March 3, 2020, from https://biblehub.com/esv/isaiah/55.htm

The Bass Handbook of Leadership: Theory, Research, and Managerial Applications. (Ch. 7 and Ch. 10): Bass, B. M. (2009). Simon & Schuster.

The Culture Map: Breaking Through the Individual Boundaries. (Ch. 10) Meyer, Erin. Pub., 2014

Meta-Psychology (Ch. 12) *Psychology: Tenth Edition in Modules*. Myers, David G. Worth Pub., 2014.

THE MOMENT LEADERS ARE BORN

RICK PEREA, Ph.D., C.P.C., C.E.P., S.I.P.

- World Champion Performance Psychologist,
- Leadership Author/Expert
- World Class Speaker &
- Champion Maker

Dr. Rick Perea practices cutting-edge performance psychology to shape performers from all walks of life. Attorneys, Athletes, Engineers, Pilots, Doctors, or anyone who wants to show up as their best version in any context. He practices at his world class performance facility, ThinkOne, in Denver, Colorado and shapes champions and everyday leaders like you and me.

His life reflects his philosophy to live at 212° every day. "Dr. P" began his career as a free-agent linebacker for the Denver Broncos and uses his wins as a college and professional football player to make a difference for athletes and teams as a psychologist. He helped the Denver Broncos win the 2016 World Super Bowl Championship focusing on the players and coach's mind-set. He has worked for the Miami Dolphins, Denver Broncos, Colorado Rockies, Denver Nuggets, Cleveland Browns, and San Antonio Spurs to name a few. He has also inspired world class organizations such as Google, Apple, and Ultimate Software Group to enhance C Suite and human capital leadership and performance. His innovative, energetic, and passionate approach changes the lives he encounters and helps shape champions for life. Learn more at www.THINKONE4YOU.ORG.

FAMILY LEGACY
#TEAM PEREA

Kaleb, Dad, & Keegan
(Drake, not present for the father/son photo, but pictured
below in family photo).

DECISION POINT

LETTER TO MY SONS

Kaleb, Keegan, & Drake:

You guys are my true dawgs! I love each of you for so many different yet equal reasons.

Kaleb (Lock): You are so disciplined and structured; you will be such a success in whatever you decide to do because, simply put: you do what you say you are going to do. I will always call you Lock (after a warlock Doberman) in my heart because of how tenacious (a true linebacker) you are. A true diplomat as well, you are so brave. Every time I see you, my heart just melts. I Love U, my brother!

Keegan (KEEKEE): You are the most eclectic adolescent I know – kindhearted, yet a badass on the football field and in life. You love people and are so accepting of other viewpoints, beliefs, and values. Handsome and fashion-conscious, you attract people of all races, ethnicities, and cultures. I love how artsy you are and how you break all the stereotypes of a true badass. Androgynous to the core; I Love U and your beautiful heart!

Drake (Acheie Drakie): You have the most beautiful smile I have ever seen! It literally not only lights up the room but my world. You dance with rhythm, sing with grace, and laugh with an uncontrollable energy. You look up to your brothers with so much respect and honor, yet you are your own person. A great basketball player, yet your brain is a true sponge that will someday spit out innovative and creative ideas that have presently not been delineated. I could hold you forever, my brother! I Love U!

Fellas: It is paramount for me to be a great father because my dad taught me responsibility and accountability. Beyond that, you three are so beautiful in your own ways. I love that level of divergence and having an eclectic stance in my family. Having a psychologist who used to play football as a father has given you a platform that is unique and somewhat esoteric. I love educating you through simple conversation when you ask me questions about school and life. But it's the lessons you teach me, that I truly value every day! We are true dawgs for life and beyond.

—Your Dad

THE TITAN: Rudolpho Victoriano Perea
From left to right: Drake, Dad, Me, Kaleb and Keegan.
This picture was taken two-months before my dad passed
away at the age of 99, in September 2019. He was
the last of the Mohicans!

MORE ABOUT THE AUTHOR

Author, speaker, teacher, and world champion performance psychologist Dr. Rick Perea is a fun and inspirational motivational speaker, radio and television spokesperson, and media expert. He is often heard on radio and TV programs as an expert in sports, psychology, and leadership.

As a keynote speaker, an expert authority in sports and business leadership, he is also adept at leading workshops, business speaking, facilitation, and special events in corporate, athletic, academic, and school environments. To invite Dr. P to speak at your next event, contact him at ThinkOne4You.org.

FOLLOW DR. P

Think One: The Behavior Design Specialist

Dr. Rick Perea, Ph.D., C.P.C., C.E.P., S.I.P.

Decision Point: The Moment Leaders Are Born

Podcast Broadcasts available at 104.3 The Fam Sports Radio, Denver

DECISION POINT

Invite Dr. Rick Perea to Speak at Your Next Event!

234